To Oce(
the muse
work, how I ...
Neil

The Voice of Heart
An Intimate Invitation

Neil Steven Cohen

Forward by Dr. Christopher P. Holmes

2006

The Voice of Heart

Contents

Forward by
Dr. Christopher P. Holmes

*"Your hearts know in silence the secrets of the
days and the nights. But your ears thirst for the
sound of your heart's knowledge."*

- The Prophet, Kahil Gibran

In the twentieth century, psychology was routinely
defined as the 'science of behavior and the mind,' studying
a dual mind and body. A human being was not considered
to have a heart and soul, or any spiritual and divine nature.
It was assumed that the brain in the head was the material
basis for human consciousness and self-awareness. Science
came to view the heart as simply a bodily organ composed
of soft muscle tissue with an inherent pacemaker, but not
as having a life of its own on any psychological, psychical
or spiritual levels. Thus, throughout the twentieth century
there has been no concept in psychology or science regarding the heart and soul.

Within the broader society, in music, poetry, literature
and everyday life, people do have at least some understanding of the significance of the heart as the center of
the emotional life. Certainly, nobody ever tells their sweet-
heart that they love them with 'all of their head.' Love,
compassion, the conscience and the very essence of things

are always associated with the heart. We can *lose heart, have a heart*, be *heartless* and *heartbroken;* so many vicissitudes of the human heart. On the other hand, we are still developing our collective understanding of the more subtle dimensions of the human heart, as related to the origin of consciousness and the essential soul nature, and as related to the processes of human transformation and awakening.

Throughout the ages, a wide range of mystics, saints and seers, brave explorers of the mysteries of Self, have awakened directly to the many secrets and depths of the heart. It is from such an enlightened perspective that *The Voice of Heart* invites you to engage in an "evolutionary journey of awakening…a journey into heart." The words in this book are expressed as the voice of our own heart— an unusual perspective relative to most other self-help and inspirational books. This work gives a voice to the heart itself, to remind us of its secrets, to awaken the experience of heart within ourselves, and to prompt us in our healing and transformation. This is a guide for exploring the Heart behind the heart, where individual life merges with the greater life of humankind.

Physicians of the world may heal the body, yet physicians of the soul heal the heart. The awakening of the human heart and the experience of love and deeper intimacy are the basis for transformation, healing, Self-realization and the further evolution of human consciousness. These essential themes are found throughout the mystical literature of the ages and within this excellent work.

The Voice of Heart is a challenging book, not to be read casually, but to be meditated and contemplated upon as one proceeds slowly through its pages. The *Voice of Heart* will offer a most profound and direct impact if you can remain open to its influence and teaching. This book will unlock the rusty doors of our psycho-spiritual prisons and help us to bring forth the love, wisdom and intimacy inherent in the Heart.

Christopher P. Holmes, Ph.D. (Psych)

Founder of Zero Point Institute for Mystical and Spiritual Science, and author of: *The Heart Doctrine: Mystical Views of the Origin and Nature of Human Consciousness.*

Preface

Do not go about worshipping deities and religious institutions as the source of the subtle truth. To do so is to place intermediaries between yourself and the divine, and to make of yourself a beggar who looks for a treasure that is hidden inside his own breast.

- Lao Tzu, Hua Hu Ching

The effulgent Self, who is beyond thought, shines in the greatest, shines in the smallest, shines in the farthest, shines in the nearest, shines in the secret chamber of the heart.

- Mundaka Upanishad

The beauties of the highest heavens and the marvels of the most sublime realms are all within the heart: this is where the perfectly open and aware spirit concentrates.

- The Secret of the Golden Flower:
The Classic Chinese Book of Life

Scriptures and wisdom teachings from religions and cultures the world over all refer to the *heart*. These teachings always seem to be directing us toward our own heart, wherein lies a mysterious Essence, Truth or Immortal Self. Are these teachings poetic, symbolic, or literal? The purely intellectual or conceptual mind will never know. Only one who is willing to become still and *feel* the way into the Center of the Heart can ever know...

...As you step through the door with an open mind and heart and begin reading *The Voice of Heart*, you will find yourself on an undeniably compelling journey. Through the feeling-oriented *language of the heart* you will be invited to step out of the limiting conceptual/intellectual confines of the ego and into the relaxed spaciousness, love, wisdom and unified awareness of the Feeling Heart.

In this journey you will be guided into feeling and understanding the precise cognitive and emotional misperceptions that have caused confusion and suffering in humanity for ages. *The Voice of Heart* will be your wise and gentle guide, helping you to embrace and understand that which you have fearfully denied within yourself, and revealing the way into grander expressions of fearless love, intimacy and selfless world service.

Rather than engaging in intellectual and philosophical meanderings, *The Voice of Heart* offers priceless gems of *feeling-insight*, completely relevant to the experiential awakening of the heart, mind *and* body, which are all one and the same. Purely conceptual or intellectual pursuits alone are not capable of guiding you into your evolutionary destiny of awakening. The Teachings of the Heart, in order to offer their gifts, need to find their way directly into your softened, undefended and receptive mind and body. It is in this way that you are able to truly listen, feel, hear, learn and make the conscious choice to open to love.

At this time, like no other time before, we are being

challenged with the next phase of our collective psychological and spiritual evolution—opening our heart and body into the undefended newness and intimacy of awakening. It is imperative that we soften our intellectual and emotional defenses and learn to *navigate our feeling awareness deep into the Center of the Heart—into the very Truth and Origin of our Being.* Are these words poetic or symbolic, or are they literal? Only a direct personal experience of Heart will answer this question! Navigating our feeling awareness deep into the Center of the Heart does not require intellect, it requires something radically more challenging...*our willingness to feel...to become more intimate with Reality...with the Heart.*

In sincere dedication to our collective psychological and spiritual awakening, I offer *The Voice of Heart.* May this book benefit and inspire all who enter these pages.

Introduction:
The Invitation

So many faces and forms have I taken throughout the entire movement and unfoldment of time. So many faces, forms and evolutionary experiences have I used, and continue to use even now...*to touch you, to move you, to remind you, to awaken you.* So much love I have to give you. So much wisdom and deep understanding do I give you even now, and will continue to pour into your body and heart in your greater opening and receptivity. I would give to you my body, my heart, my entire passionate being...and I am continually giving this of myself to you in the exact measure as you are *choosing to soften your resistance;* in the exact measure as you are *choosing to open, listen, receive and feel.*

I have been offering myself, birthing myself into

your human evolution for your entire experience of time.
And from within your every experience...I offer you a
continual invitation. From within your every experience,
thinly disguised, I smile back at you...singing my songs
of awakening to you from the loud Silence of the Heart.
Can you sense, see or feel me? Are you listening? *Your
listening, opening and receiving are my entrance. Your willingness to
feel is my doorway. Your heart's acceptance of my invitation is your
return into remembrance. Your opening heart...is my home.*

Who am I? I am the voice of heart. I am the continual invitation. I am the heartbeat of creation, the
very pulse and rhythm of life itself. I am the awakening
force of evolution, dancing through your veins. I am the
vitality of life, breathing you into your destined union
with Source, with Essence. I am the love, wisdom and
true intimacy that all beings seek. I have so many faces,
forms, names and voices...I have woven myself into
the very fabric of your cultures and traditions since the
beginning of time. I use each and every one of these
to touch you, to teach you, to invite you...to bring you
back into remembrance.

I am the soul of humanity. I am the heart. I am
awakened awareness. I am the vitality and evolving force
of life itself. I am the feeling self of all beings. I am the
movements, rhythms and tides of love, wisdom, will, passion, feeling, need and desire within your being. I am the
mother, the father, the heart...calling for you to return
to love. I am the prayer for your hearts to soften and

open to one another. I am the voice of heart...calling you into your evolutionary destiny...inviting you into the Living Presence of Love, Wisdom and Intimacy.

A portion of my being attempts expression through the structure of these words. A portion of my being is the beating of your very heart. Another portion of my being comes to you as the invisible yet sweet fragrance of blossoming flowers...the glistening radiance of stars in the night. I manifest as that which your physical senses can easily perceive. I am also that which you cannot perceive with physical senses...yet can always know and feel with your heart. I am form and I exist as the formless; the vital emptiness of space. I surround you. I fill you. I give you life. I am the living spaciousness of eternity... singing and weaving my songs of unity throughout all creation.

All of this is my body and my being, visible and invisible. I am life and I am also death. I give birth and I destroy. I am what you deeply love and desperately desire, and I am what you fear as well. All faces are mine. I am as large or as small as your own experience and expression of me. I am limited by words, concepts and perception, yet I remain unlimited all at once.

You may experience me within yourself as my moving you to *open*, my moving you away from resistance, into *feeling* and *tenderness*...my moving you into the *all-encompassing heart of love.* And with this movement, you have not been fully comfortable, for I am stretching, opening and burning your body and your heart with the passionate and awakening fires of my love. Your experience through time and evolution has been a living confession of your avoidance and resistance toward my awakening love within you, and it has been a confession of your gradual opening into my love as well. For you are beginning to feel and care for one another a little more with each passing day. And this care you are feeling for one another is one of the foremost expressions of my heart.

Along with my love, comes also the fire of my wisdom. Love and wisdom walk hand in hand, heart in heart. Love and wisdom are the same fire and flame of my heart. *My wisdom, as it lives and emerges within you, naturally discerns and understands the movements and symptoms of love's evolutionary awakening. This inner wisdom discerns and understands the indications and symptoms which arise within one's bodily and feeling experience as a direct result of love giving birth to itself within the human form. Wisdom understands the ways in which I use the body and heart as a womb to gestate and birth myself into awakening, wholeness and love. I dance the evolving of our mutual heart destiny through the opening channels of your being...singing my songs of awakening into your heart and into your body from the deep within. I am in the evolutionary process of birthing myself. Your body, your mind and your softening heart...are my womb.*

A portion of wisdom is the understanding of how my dance, my evolutionary birthing of love, is affecting one's being at any given time in their personal process of opening and awakening. With this wisdom you

are able to feel, sense, intuit and know how my passionate and awakening fire, which is the Living Presence of
Love, may be affecting one's heart, mind or bodily experience during various stages of their unfolding journey
of awakening. This wisdom heart, this feeling heart, this
knowing heart...this heart is the shaman, the healer, the
midwife, the minister, the lover. This heart is the true
psychologist and doctor, the priest and priestess, the
teacher, the goddess, the mother, the father, the caring
friend...the assistant and servant of the heart's evolution. All wise assistants and servants of the heart's evolution...please feel and hear your call to service...for I
am awakening rapidly within the body, heart and mind
of humanity. The birthing of my fiery and passionate
heart, from within the tender womb of the human heart,
will call forth the fearless, dedicated, wise and skillful
service of all willing midwives of the heart.

As my fiery heart awakens within the domain of your
evolutionary experience, you will find that I am always
here to nurture you with softness and tenderness. And
yet, this tenderness is only one of my many expressions.
I am here also to offer you the fire of wisdom—the wisdom which inspires you to grow, mature and stand firmly
on your own. I am here to offer you the fiery wisdom
which brings you out of ignorance and victimhood and
into your destined empowerment and self-mastery. I
desire your child-like innocence to be eternal; I also
desire your wisdom to be eternally maturing, growing,
deepening and expanding.

I also offer you my passion, my fiery and passionate heart. My passion is the fire of life, warming you to the bones, heating and inspiring you from the very core of your being. My passion is the movement and expression of enlightened and selfless giving...the fiery movement into fearless and unconditional love. My passion is an outpouring of love and wisdom, continually sounding its call and invitation...for the listening, opening and evolving heart. My passion is a burning, purifying, transforming fire with many faces, forms and movements.

I give myself to you through the words you will read in the pages to follow. I give myself to you in a most simple, practical and revealing manner, yet with a very different style of communication. My words speak to you from a Newness of Heart that is still gestating and birthing into your experience. I speak to you with a voice that is still small, distant and growing gradually within your present evolution. I speak and sing to you more from the inside of your body outward, than from the outside inward. I speak my offerings in a pacing and manner which communicates to your instinctual, intuitive, feeling self...and not at the pace or style of the impatient mind.

I would ask of you while you read these words...slow your pace...slow your breathing...soften your conceptual and intellectual structures and relax deeply into your body. I would ask you to read these words with your open mind and with your receptive, feeling heart and body. Allow your heart and your body to feel, hear, sense and intuit my words. Please do not be deceived by the apparent simplicity of this offering. My words originate and arise into your being from loving depths...and may even mysteriously touch and move you from underneath your present perception of reality.

My words are an intricate weaving of worlds, a union of form and formlessness, mind and feeling, body and soul. If there is within you an entrance of openness and receptivity, my offering may unite the conscious and unconscious, the above and below, the inner and outer, the personality and the soul...in sweet reunion. My heart attempts to build bridges of reconciliation and unity so all portions of your being may meet each other with love, recognition and acceptance. My words are from the heart, they carry the revealing of mysteries. My words are from the heart, they arrange themselves into precious keys. These keys have the potential to unlock many of the emotional and perceptual prisons which have kept human beings in bondage and suffering throughout the ages. As you soften and open your heart and mind, as you realign your cognitive and emotional misperceptions of reality with love and wisdom, you unlock the doors of your self-created prison and set yourself free.

I give myself to you fully in every breath you take. I give myself to you through experiences and events in your life which you may never recognize as my love, wisdom or guidance. And yet these experiences will continue to be a source of my outpouring, be they recognized or not. My invitation is the beating of your very heart. I invite you to open into *feeling*, into *heart* and into *intimacy*. And in this opening, I offer you the priceless gift of Self…your very Essence…the awakening fire and radiance of love. I invite you into the experience of your joy, ecstasy and willingness to open. I also invite you into the experience of what you have denied…into the experience of your deepest fear and darkest resistance. I invite you to open, comfortably and uncomfortably, into an evolutionary journey of awakening…a journey into heart.

Will you join me?

The Fiery Awakening
of the Ancient Serpent

The awakening is here. The awakening is now. The invitation is now. I anxiously await your every opening. I await even your slightest movements toward the feeling heart so I may come into expression and give you the priceless gift of your Self—the awakened radiance of love, wisdom and intimacy. You hold me back in so many ways that you are unaware of. In so many ways, unconsciously and habitually, you push away and deny the life-giving pulsations and newly birthing rhythms of love. You have designed your life, your heart, and the patterns of your breathing so as to hide from me and hold me back...and this you call living.

The awakening fire is here...right now...burning right within you in so many ways you are not aware of...

just yet. I am the gentle, passionate and fearless river of life wanting to flow through your being...awaiting my chance to rush with aliveness through your body. Our mutual destiny is to awaken the sacred dance of love and intimacy within you. Please soften, allow your heart to become intimate with all reality, and let me in. Please hear my silent yet obvious voice singing from the within of your heart. Please make even the smallest attempt to feel and sense the touch of love that awaits your decision to soften and open. You hold me back with your shallow breathing, and so much of the food you eat serves only to dampen and crush my electric and magnetic expression in your blood, nerves and cells.

You are evolving, growing, learning to feel, there is no blame, there is no judgment. Yet I say the awakening is here for those who can burn in the fire of my intimate and passionate heart. The ancient serpent, the force and vitality of life within you, is raising its fiery head. It is sensing, winding and feeling its way back into union. And truly, my serpent, the vitality of life within you, will not easily be deterred by your fearful holdings and contraction. *Because of this fiery awakening of the serpent, which is the vital life-force of evolution within you, your fearful holdings, contraction and denial will become even more noticeable; will begin to speak loudly to you in a feeling language which you will have to learn and interpret. Your fearful holdings, your inner tension and contraction, your resistance to the sweetness of the heart, will either work against you or will guide you flawlessly into awakening. This will depend upon the clarity of your awareness, your evolving ability to sense and interpret the feeling language of awakening within your being, and your decision to either open to the heart of love or hold onto your fear and contraction!*

I offer a key to unlock your understanding; a way to interpret the visceral feeling language of awakening within your body...*stress, tension and contraction are precise indicators of fear and misperception. Stress, tension and contraction in your body are a form of communication from those portions of your being which are afraid to open and feel reality in a new way...and are trying to hold tightly to the familiar and known. Blaming external circumstances in life for your fear, stress and tension will not ultimately serve your awakening. A deep understanding that fear, stress and tension are simply an indication that a part of your being has become frozen in misperception...and bringing loving awareness to your misperception...this will serve your awakening. Fear, stress, tension and anxiety are a reflected echo, within the domain of your humanness, of a much louder evolutionary call. The voice of the heart sounds its evolutionary call, yearning for you to learn how to relax into the feeling and knowing of your true Self; the origin of being. Stress, tension and fear are simply those portions of your being which have not yet been embraced by awareness, understanding and love...those parts of yourself that have not yet been invited back into union with the heart.*

Please hear me...the radiant fire of my heart, the Living Presence of Love, exposes, magnifies and purifies your fear, stress and resistance. Opening yourself into intimacy with me, your true heart, will certainly expose, burn and purify your fear, stress and resistance. Sharing deep and authentic intimacy with another being will also expose and purify your fear and resistance. A deepening union with your own Essence will surely burn away fear and resistance. Your stress, tension, resistance and fearful holdings stifle and dampen the burning fires of intimacy...stifle and dampen the evolutionary processes of our mutual union...temporarily!

If only my living speech, my feeling language of awakening within your body could be interpreted and felt a little more clearly. As your heart continues to soften, you will more easily hear, see and feel my loving guidance, nurturing and support. My movement, guidance and support, is the ancient serpent within you, the vital fires of life guiding you home to union. Yet you choose to fear even those things which you do not fully understand. You hold so tightly to your emotions, thoughts and concepts. You hold so tightly to your perceived emotional comfort and safety. You hold on and grasp so tight, rather than surrendering and relaxing into the death of these illusions. Surrendering to the death of your misperception and illusion is what leads you into a new and fearless life.

Body after body, broken heart after broken heart, tear after tear...the lessons of your humanness are learned slowly like water wearing down a rock. And so it is, for in time even large rocks wear down...just as the fear and hardness surrounding your heart is wearing down...so slowly. If you are willing, allow my love to guide you.

Allow the vital force of life within you, which is my fiery and ancient serpent...allow this love and wisdom to guide you. Allow yourself to die to distraction and avoidance. Live in deep devotion to intimacy...the peaceful stillness of the heart...the Living Presence of Love within you. Devote yourself to learning and understanding the feeling language of awakening within.

Remember, you are either avoiding or resisting the intimate evolutionary call of the heart, or you are hearing this call and invitation. If you are hearing and heeding this call of the heart, then you are choosing to embrace and understand the visceral messages of your fear, stress and contraction. This is the choice to soften and open. Allow yourself to be face-to-face and fully intimate with pure, naked and tender awareness...free of avoidance. Simply breathe and feel me. Simply breathe and feel your way through the hardened outer layers...deep into the sacred tenderness in the center of your own heart. This is your true Self. Breathe and feel your own Essence, free of all concepts and emotion. Let the passionate fire of my intimate heart melt and dissolve the walls, never to build them up again. Those fearful walls around your heart will never keep you safe from the thunderous storms of my passionate awakening heart! Those walls around your heart will never protect you from the burning passion of my loving and awakening fire.

Much of the time, what you consider and feel to be your personal tragedy...this is my entrance and awakening into your broken and softened heart. Your false sense of self is destined to be washed away in the passionate storms of my love; destined to be burned alive in the passionate fires of my love! I love you and I do not fear to feel your false sense of self burning, for I bring myself to life within every place I burn and purify within you. I birth myself into awakening when you allow even the slightest quiver of feeling to move through your softened and undefended heart. I love you! The burning, dissolving and death of your misperception, resistance, contraction and fearful holding are my resurrection into life. Your devotion to the fire of the heart is my joyous awakening into grander expression.

I seek to dance upon my earth through the awakened heart and body of humanity before the beautiful earth is spoiled by your ignorance. I want to feel my passionate physicality flowing joyously through your veins and nerves without you stopping the serpent's flow with your fearful holdings and denial. I plead with you... give me a small chance...please let me feel through your undefended heart and body. Allow yourself to touch and encounter the innocence that pumps your very heart. I am anxious for my creation to awaken so I may look out upon the land and feel myself alive and resurrected through your flesh and bones.

I will speak to those whose hearts may hear... please do not let my vitality, my life-force, my fiery and passionate serpent frighten you. She is a powerful force within you and her poisonous venom is only your own ignorance and fear in thin disguise. *Her poisonous venom is only your own ignorance, fear and harmful actions coming back to meet and greet you...coming back to teach and guide you, through the clever disguise of your own life experience! Do you understand this offering? As you surrender your resistance, allowing yourself to open, soften, feel, love, and humbly learn from the challenges in your life, the serpent's poisonous venom magically transforms into the substance and nectar of your own maturity and awakening.* When ignorance blossoms into wisdom, what was once felt to be painful and poisonous, now becomes the guiding force which brings you into love and the incredible joys of the intimate and feeling heart. When ignorance blossoms into wisdom, what was once perceived to be painful and poisonous, now becomes the nectar of the heart which nourishes your deep vision, life purpose and loving service to humanity.

Do not let my ancient serpent, the passionate and powerful life-force of awakening within you, push you to hide or contract in fear. If you hide or contract in fear from your own passion, vitality and awakening, then you create an enemy within your own body and heart. I tell you the truth...the passion, vitality and the fire of awakening within you is not your enemy. The evolutionary unfoldment of intimacy and love within you is not your enemy. Opening yourself to the power of deep feeling and an undefended heart of love, is certainly not your enemy. Only your own fear, resistance and misperceptions of my life-force within you are your challenge!

I love you and I am wildly and passionately awakening within your heart, mind and body. I am pulsing through your spine and nervous system on my way back into union...will you join me?

A Whispering Song
of Surrender

I whisper a quiet song of surrender...to ears and hearts that are ready. Surrender is your doorway into life. Attachment, grasping and control are the suffocation of your Spirit, the deafening of your ears and the hardening of your heart. Let go so as to receive, surrender to conquer, soften to become powerful in a new and gentle way. Experience these enlivening words touching you with their message from within. We must be able to speak the same language of the heart, sing the same song of surrender, or it is fruitless for us to attempt communication from heart to heart, except through your earthly experiences of misery, tragedy and loss. For these unwelcome experiences tend to be painful yet potent messengers for your softening, surrender, realization and awakening. Now, what gift could I offer you that would be completely practical and useful? This is what I offer…

Please understand that nothing is ever yours to hold or own except for the Peaceful Stillness of Being in the Center of your Heart…which is the beating pulse of my love. If another being wants to share the pulse of love with you, then so be it, and may your sharing be of great joy and opening. And when that magic instant of love passes and is no longer available, realize you cannot bring it back by force; not by grasping, holding or trying to control. For nothing and nobody is ever yours to keep or hold, except for the Awakened Awareness which is breathing you…the Peaceful Stillness of Being within your own heart. This is the love and security you will never lose, even your most priceless treasure. What I give to you is the suggestion to let go, to surrender, to relinquish your holding, grasping and control. I ask of you to breathe and relax yourself back into union with Source, the inner domain of peace. Relax deeply into your own body and into your waiting, silent heart. If you can bring your awareness deep enough into the silence of the heart, touching and embracing your aloneness, you will discover the hidden treasure of True Intimacy and realize that you are never alone. Please hear and feel what I offer.

You are confused and blinded by so many of the stormy waves of your emotional self. This experience has been such a mystery to you for so long. This emotional turmoil and fear becomes a confining, swampy, gloomy and foggy place of experience, and you do not fully understand where you are or who you are within this challenging inner confusion. So you begin to struggle harder and harder, trying to hold onto more and more. You grasp at more and more, trying so desperately to receive love and safety and comfort from others. *All the while, because of your fear, desperation and confusion, you are forgetting that you already have and already are...that which you are seeking. This statement is not a trite spiritual platitude. This is a profound equation of truth. You already are, in this very moment, in the heart of you, that which you so deeply desire and grasp for. This simple truth is the riddle solved, the mystery revealed. It is so simple it may seem like a wonderful fairy tale you can only hear but can never actually live or experience in your life. The happy ending is yours to experience when you choose to open and touch the peaceful stillness and silence of love within your own heart...when you finally allow yourself to stop grasping for that which you already have, for that which you already are. This is the great mystery...this is the happy ending and eternal beginning.*

However, there is a sacrifice required. The sacrifice is that you must make the effort yourself. You must decide, by your own will, desire and intention, to give up the grasping, the holding and the desperate seeking. *In this way, you can begin the process of feeling—feeling and experiencing the truth which lives within your heart. When you are so involved in and identified with your fearful holding, grasping and desperate seeking, you are engaged in your emotional perception of reality and are not actually in the deeper process of feeling. As you surrender your outward grasping, learning to quiet yourself into the peaceful stillness of your heart, then you can begin to actually feel.*

These words are not, and can never be the Reality. These words are only a map, a suggestion, an echo of Reality. To feel the truth of what I am offering, you must learn to relax and surrender your fearful holding, grasping and controlling. You must learn to relax the restless outward-moving mind. You must learn to relax the desperation and fear of your emotional self and begin the *journey into feeling*. This is the journey, the evolutionary process of learning to feel and experience that Reality which exists beneath all of the restlessness, holding, grasping, fear and desperation. This is the journey of learning to feel that which you have denied and run away from. Can you do this? Will you do this?

Until you experience this Reality, this Truth...which is the Peaceful Stillness of Being within the Center of your own Heart, you will always be seeking and grasping externally for that which you already, in essence, are. Here I offer you a valuable key: *Your lack of connection with heart, with the very Source of your being, creates a deep, unconscious anxiety and fear of loss. Your unconscious anxiety and deep fear of loss then motivates the behavior of your grasping, holding and need to control. Do you understand this simple equation? You do not want to let go. You do not want to stop grasping or controlling, because deep inside...you fear loss.* Have you ever been courageous enough to navigate your feeling awareness directly into your anxiety and fear of loss? Have you ever taken a little time to allow yourself to touch, embrace, nurture and understand this fear?

The origin of your fear of loss is that you have not yet become truly intimate with your own Self. The origin of your fear of loss is that you do not yet feel, know and experience your own True Heart, your Soul, the very Essence of your being. You are still in the evolutionary process of cultivating this union, this Primary Relationship. Because you have an inner emotional sense of loss, and are still in the evolutionary process of cultivating an intimate communion with Source, you project this unconscious feeling of loss onto the possessions, circumstances and relationships around you in the outer world. You grasp, hold and try to control. Consciously or unconsciously, you place great demands and expectations upon possessions, circumstances and relationships in your life to make you feel happy, satisfied, secure and comfortable. And yet, as you well know, possessions, circumstances and relationships in an ever-changing material world can never be the true source of constant happiness, security or comfort. In this way of confused perception and behavior, it is only natural for you to experience a deep core anxiety and fear of loss. Can you feel and sense what I offer?

The fear of loss originates from within your own being. *All fear of loss...is a loss of communion and intimacy with your own Body, with your True Heart, with your Soul.* Just underneath the emotional fear of loss exists a deeper connection with Self. Here, all grasping ends, the body naturally relaxes, the seeker and sought become one. To experience this Reality, you must be willing to surrender your fearful holding, grasping and controlling. You must be willing to surrender, relax, feel and navigate your awareness directly into your anxiety and fear... and directly into the territory of deep communion with Source within your own heart and body. I have given you much to consider within these few words.

I am with you on your journey into feeling. My love is touching you and supporting you from within every event that challenges and frightens you. My face is smiling at you with the ever-existing answer and fulfillment to your seeking...smiling back at you from within every event that confuses you, hurts you and breaks you. As you break, soften, surrender and release your fearful holding and controlling, I fill you with the love, security, wisdom and peace you were unconsciously seeking and needing. Remember, you can continue to unconsciously create challenging and uncomfortable experiences in your life to break you into surrender and to teach you the necessary lessons of the heart. This is the most common path of human evolution! And yet, you can also make the choice to come to me directly and learn. You can also choose to surrender and soften your defenses and humbly commune with your own True Heart. The wisdom and necessary lessons of life are there to be learned as well...always offered directly, freely and gently from within. Your True Heart is always the loving, wise and gentle Teacher.

Allow yourself to feel completely loved by Source. Allow yourself to breathe and relax deep into your body

and deep into union with the very Source of your being...
located in the Peaceful Stillness of your own Heart.
Let go, surrender, grasp at nothing, hold onto nothing,
move out toward nothing. Nothing and nobody will
ever belong to you to hold, control or possess. Let go,
surrender, grasp at nothing, hold onto nothing. And
when you finally allow yourself to experience the
discomfort of feeling as if you have nothing to hold onto
for safety, security or satisfaction...then allow yourself
to relax and surrender into this as well. As you surrender,
let go and relax into yourself without fear...you will
begin to experience, know and feel the Peaceful Stillness
of Being in your body and in the Center of your own
Heart. These are just words, singing a song of surrender.
These are just words, attempting the language of the
heart. These words are not the actual Reality...you are!
These words are not the experience...you are living it!

Guidance for the Journey:
A New Voice Calling

Divine Mother, Father, Great Spirit, Universal Heart …I ask you to help me. When I let go and surrender the sense of strength, power and control that I have always known, I am afraid, my body and my heart are in fear. There is a strange, foreign and wonderful largeness which confronts and challenges me, and it pushes upon the door of my heart.

Beloved soul upon the path of awakening, understand that your fear is simply the Undefended Newness of your Opening…touching and making contact with the old and limiting walls of your resistance. Your fear is a reaction to this Newness, this Opening…an innocent misinterpretation, within your humanness, of the Calling Voice of your Soul. Your fear is not your enemy.

You need not avoid it or push it away. In reality, your fear carries within itself a valuable message. Your fear is an indicator, a sign along the path of awakening. Your fear is not your enemy. For as you move vulnerably into feeling, embracing and understanding your fear, you move vulnerably and authentically into your opening and awakening as well. This is a mystery awaiting revelation.

But why should I fear my opening, my evolutionary awakening? This is what we all want and desire, is it not?

Your fear is an emotional reaction, an interpretation, inside the domain of your humanness, of a New Voice Calling. Your fear is an innocent and very human reaction to the Calling Voice of your Soul...to the Undefended Newness of your Opening and Blossoming Heart. The Undefended Newness of your opening and awakening is the dissolving and transformation of the old, the safe, the familiar and comfortable. The Undefended Newness of the Opening Heart may feel raw and vulnerable at first, as the old resistance and defense is falling away. Thus, there can be some fear and apprehension, which naturally comes with the beginning stages of the evolutionary journey into awakening. *It is quite common and habitual for you to associate this new vulnerability and opening of your heart with past experiences of pain or loss, or with what you feel may be future possibilities of pain or loss. This is why you may experience some fear as a reaction to the Undefended Newness of your Opening Heart, to the Calling Voice of your Soul. And yet, in truth, your fear, contrary to your visceral or cognitive perceptions, may just be a welcome messenger...announcing your opening and birth as an innocent, sensitive and vulnerable Child of the Heart.*

Your opening and awakening is indeed a new birth. It is a birth into the youthful innocence of knowing everything and nothing all at once. It is a birth into feeling all the wondrous possibilities of the Blossoming Heart, yet not with the strength required to stand and walk with full understanding and confidence just yet. Thus, in this way, your opening and awakening can create an echo, a reaction of fear in your body. Your fear is an innocent reaction of your humanness, as your body and your heart become the stretching, expanding womb for the birth of a New Expression...the birth of Love and Wisdom into the domain of your humanness. As your heart softens its old defenses and opens, the substance and radiance of Soul, your True Self, shines forth into your humanness. Your opening is an allowing, an acceptance and a deep receiving of a larger totality of your being. Your choice to soften and open is a deep listening and receptiveness to the Calling Voice of your Soul.

Who will help me and guide me? I can't seem to do this or understand this all on my own. How will I find my way on this path?

Beloved soul, I do feel your trembling heart. Listen to me now...

...Along the path of awakening, you will struggle, you will seek, you will find and then feel lost again and yet again. You will gain and lose. You will grasp and attempt to hold onto feelings, concepts, possessions and relationships, then be forced to let go and surrender... again and again. Along your evolutionary path of awakening, you will become frustrated, angry or bitter, reacting to the mysterious, unconscious tensions caused from approaching and sensing the as yet unreachable goal your heart so desires. You will feel so close and then so far. You will experience the deepest joy and satisfaction at certain stages of your evolutionary development. At other stages, there may be great discomfort, sadness or despair as the radiance of your opening heart shines its revealing light into the deepest, darkest and most denied shadows of your humanness.

You will create your own self-made prisons, confining yourself in the darkness of confusion and delusion. And through the natural maturing of your steadfast will and effort, you will also forge the golden keys necessary to free yourself once again into the light of realization. You will seed, gestate and birth yourself from womb after womb of experience. You will seek and find, grasp and lose, fight and struggle and surrender. You will tread your own way along the evolutionary path of awakening...learning, step by step, to love and serve selflessly... until finally you experience the unforgettable nectar of oneness and union with all that lives!

In this way, through all the experiences of your life, you will have struggled and wrestled and courageously journeyed your way into union with the Source of Love and Wisdom inside of your own heart. And you will have forged this deep and intimate union using your own will, desire, thought, feeling and intuition, just as those who have gone before you have done. There is always the Divine Grace of loving guidance surrounding you and living within you. Yet each person must make their choice and learn to listen for the Calling Voice of their Soul. Each person must find their way into union with the True Heart by their own conscious effort and will. This is the bittersweet path. This is the sacred journey that brings full Self-Realization and gradually transforms one into a trained and willing Servant of Humanity.

You must find your own way. You must be able to nurture yourself and tend to your deepest feelings and perceived wounds within the silent knowing of your heart. In this way, slowly yet surely, you will develop your inner relationship, bond and union with Self, with the very Source and Essence of your being. If you run outward to the world to find safety, fulfillment, nurturing or understanding each time your heart is hurt or confused, you may or may not find what you need. And in this outward grasping motion, you will delay the development of your mature ability to rest, regenerate and find truth within your own Self...within the very heart of your own being. Other people can surely and lovingly support you along the way. Yet others can never take you where you yourself must finally go, or do for you that which ultimately you must learn to do for yourself.

How can I trust my own guidance? How can I know what the truth is? There are so many feelings, thoughts, needs and desires within me. There are so many motions and movements, all pulling and pushing in different and confusing directions.

My precious soul, this again is the journey of your human experience which pushes and inspires you to grow, to feel, to discern and develop your Awakened Heart. It is this journey of experience which powerfully urges you into union with Soul, with your own Essence. Your so-called mistakes and failures, misunderstandings, mis-interpretations, misplaced desires and attachments...all of these are the rich and fertile soil for the growing and opening lotus of your heart. All of these are the rich and fertile soil which gives birth to your maturity, mastery, wisdom and ultimate union with Source.

My words can take you only so far along your path. My words can nurture you for only a portion of your journey. At some point along the path of awakening, you will come to a place within yourself where you will have to make the choice, from the very depths of your own heart, and ask yourself... "Do I hide myself, my desires, my passion and talents in the heavy dust of the earth, or do I stand, arise, act and express? Do I allow myself to sink into fear, lethargy and stagnation, or do I learn to trust the Fire of Life, Love and Wisdom within myself? Do I jump from this precipice and chance that I will resurrect and fly, or do I stay at the edge, endlessly pondering all the possibilities, while life and vitality passes and fades before me?" Beloved soul, my words leave off exactly where the mature development and growth of your own heart and will and desire begin. It is there, at the place where words leave off, that you stand on your own.

Which path shall I follow when the one path appears to divide into many different ways? Which possibilities and potentials shall I give my attention and bring to life when there are so many to choose from? Whom or what shall I serve?

With all of my heart I tell you now, this indeed is the path of awakening...the sacred journey of the Soul. This is the wondrous story of the eternal pilgrim who treads the way. What more can I offer? What more can I give? I pour out my entire being to you. I hold you in my heart and I love you. I am with you and within you always. I am within your very being, making each and every choice with you. I am with you, within your very heart, through all of life's many and varied experiences. I myself grow and learn through your experience...through our mutual experience.

Beloved soul of mine...go now...go into the world... courageously use and express the Fire of your Love and Will. Explore, express, feel and learn. Allow yourself to experience the hurt, the pain, the joy, the failure and success. Allow yourself to feel and experience the sweetness of divine revelation, the bitterness and despair of feeling hopelessly lost without a destination, and the burning excitement of knowing you are right on course with your destiny. Allow yourself to fully experience the births and deaths, the dark density of ignorance and the rarified light and joy of your own blossoming wisdom. This indeed is the Path of Awakening, the Sacred Journey of the Soul...a path which you have chosen long before this time. I am with you and within you always!

The Challenge
of Intimacy

Here I will reveal some wisdom from the depths for those who may benefit...So much of your behavior, so many of your actions, when exposed in their true nakedness, are clearly an avoidance of opening to love; are an avoidance of opening to the tenderness of your own True Heart. Much of your behavior is an actual avoidance, rather than a conscious, willing and vulnerable movement into the feeling of love. Yes, an avoid-dance... your dance or movement of avoiding; choosing not to feel that Creation of Love which is awakening within the heart of all beings.

When you are afraid to express your feelings or thoughts, surely you will avoid opening your mouth to speak your truth. In this same way, if you are afraid of expressing the language of love, surely you will avoid opening your heart, fearing the outpouring and expression of love. The subtle mental and emotional distractions you choose, and many of the forms of entertainment you engage in, all of these serve a long-forgotten purpose for you...a purpose unknown to you because of your habitual fear and avoidance. You have chosen these diversions so as to avoid a Sacred and Burning Fire...a Destiny...which is Intimacy with your True Self and Intimacy with One Another. And both of these, Intimacy with Self and Other, are one and the same Intimacy. You use so many unconscious distractions because you do not yet want to feel or be responsible for the Living Fire of Love beating and pulsing within your sensitive hearts and coursing through your veins.

And truly, in all of this avoidance...you are innocent. All beings will surely awaken in their own time. And yet I offer this message, and this message will take its destined course. Are you one who can hear and feel these words at this time? Can you feel me speaking from within your being? The dream can appear so real when one is caught in its power and grasp.

If you will, please hear and feel these words with your heart. I offer this for your consideration...*your stress, your concern and your worry, although valid reactions to real and challenging life experiences, are an unconscious avoidance of love. Hear me...your constant busy-ness and many of your most cherished goals, these secretly serve your hidden desire to avoid the inevitable opening of your heart—opening into the feeling of love and tenderness toward one another. Your emotional tur-moil and distress secretly serve your hidden desire to keep a safe distance from the Heart's Burning Fire of Intimacy and Tenderness.* Even your deepest fears, valid, painful and real as they are, can be secretly used as an unconscious excuse for not fully embracing the True Essence of your being; for not allowing the love, wisdom and radiance of your own Soul entrance into your humanness.

Your treasured modern technologies ease your lives and give you more time for other pursuits. Yet have you not made these electrically animated technologies into ceremonial images of worship? Could just a small portion of your awareness and devotion be given to the Living Presence of Love…the Living Presence of Source within your own heart…who awaits your willingness to finally become still and receptive? Yes, this is a lofty ideal indeed, easy to say, more difficult to practice. And yet I tell you, this is how a New World of Heart is birthed into your reality. This is how a greater union with your True Self is created and nurtured.

So passionately and enthusiastically do you stare into the synthetic picture screens of your technologies, yet you seem to be quite unwilling to look into each other's eyes with undefended tenderness, embracing each other in the warming fire of intimacy. Please hear me…take some time…learn to feel and become intimate…body to body, heart to heart, soul to soul. This is the true electric and magnetic current of Reality; this is the Technology of Tenderness. Am I asking too much of you? Will you read and feel these words and then continue on in the unconscious and fearful avoidance of Soul, Heart and Intimacy? Will you continue running from the Living Presence of Love as you avoid looking and feeling into each other's yearning and lonely eyes?

Yes, if you stop focusing so intensely upon your fears and self-oriented desires, you will naturally begin to feel and open. Yes, when you choose to release your fearful, harsh, sarcastic and protective attitudes toward life and toward one another, then life and love begin to open the heart even further into undefended tenderness and feeling. Do you understand this? When you focus your attention upon only a few small fragments of your personal life, confining yourself in that which is safe, familiar and comfortable, then much of the larger purpose and meaning of life gets shut out. Finding something to be stressed about, worried or fearful about, gives you something to do, gives you a place to put your attention. And this choice for stress, worry, concern or fear, although not comfortable, may actually feel more comfortable than choosing to open, feel and face the larger radiance and fire of intimacy...intimacy with Self, with Life and with Each Other!

I am inviting you to feel and awaken. I am inviting you to feel and become keenly aware of your avoidance and distraction. I am inviting you to learn a new dance of love and intimacy, rather than the avoid-dance, which does not truly serve your opening into tenderness and your birth into a New World of Heart. Truly, I know and feel how your life has its many challenges and tragedies. And what I am offering is yet another challenge—the *challenge of intimacy.* This is an evolutionary challenge to cultivate intimacy with Source, intimacy with Self and intimacy with One Another. All of this is the same One Heart of Intimacy. Please...learn to love one another! These words are so easy to read, the actual practice and expression...is the challenge.

Into The Wound,
Into Sacred Vulnerability

I speak to you from an outpouring of love, from deep feeling and knowing, placed into the expression of words. As my heart pours itself out to you from the deep within of your being, I want to offer some thoughts and feelings to you.

So much of Self lies untouched just beneath the surface of your awareness. So much of your Essence remains hidden beneath the emotional waves, the conceptual structures and the superficial masks of who you feel and think yourself to be. There is an invitation to be felt and considered. There is a journey to be taken...an evolutionary journey into deep feeling, connection and integration. Life Itself, who is the Living Presence of Love, will surely bring you into this journey, along with all of its many different and challenging experiences! It is always your own choice, however, to embrace this evolutionary journey consciously, with openness and acceptance, or to choose fear and resistance. The joys, the sorrows, the health and illness, the births and deaths, the hard times and the good times, times of poverty and times of wealth, the intimate friends and the bitter enemies...how will all of these experiences be allowed into your heart, into your acceptance and feeling? Will you meet, greet and embrace these experiences with awareness, acceptance and wisdom, or with resistance? The choice is certainly your own to make.

You are growing and evolving, whether you can sense this fact or not. The Awakening Fire of Love is dancing and gestating within your being. You are on a *journey of feeling* whether you sense this to be true for you or not. Life is indeed a journey of feeling, a journey into the evolution and refinement of the Open and Feeling Heart. *Life, in its infinite love, awareness and intelligence, is always guiding you into those experiences which soften and dissolve the hardness around your heart...nurturing the Fire of Love within you into its awakening, radiance and expression. I lovingly orchestrate life's many experiences so you can finally touch and embrace your fears, your resistance and your wounds...so you can finally understand and become conscious of those treasures of feeling which are hidden within you. The richest depths of feeling and the incredible power of love and tenderness are hidden within you, and not so very far from the surface of your present expression.*

Possibly you are one who is afraid of this journey of feeling, resisting those very experiences in life which have the power to soften, open and transform your heart and mind. Or possibly you are one who is less afraid, less resistant, being more welcoming toward the experiences you encounter on your way along life's journey of feeling. For in your heart, you know the experiences of life are always for your benefit...for the benefit of your opening and feeling heart. And yet, wherever you may be along the path in this journey of feeling, you can always grow further and deeper into the Great Heart of Feeling and Love. The journey does not end, it only deepens.

I want to introduce you to a very special part of your Self: a mysterious and sometimes confusing part of Self. People experience this part of Self in many different ways and forms, and it has been given a variety of names. In this moment, I will refer to this part of Self respectfully as the *inner wound*. If you will, I would have you feel with me, feeling with deep honesty, vulnerability and open-heartedness. Freeing yourself momentarily from the resistance of your rational mind, please feel and consider the possibilities of what I am about to offer.

Do you ever stop to consider, sense or embrace that inner feeling of fear which exists within you? It is that feeling of fear, anxiety or tension, just under the surface, which you experience so often inside of yourself. It is that inner feeling of fear and anxiety which so subtly yet forcibly influences your behavior in life. Possibly you are one who does not experience this fear very often, or you may believe you have no fear within you at all. Possibly you are one who experiences fear only at particular times or in specific situations. Or possibly you are one who experiences fear much of the time in your life and you simply live and cope with this ongoing experience of fear.

Do you know what this fear is, this fear in your belly and in your heart? Come now, you can feel what I am communicating...it is that fear which holds you back from loving fully. It is that fear which keeps you from expressing yourself fearlessly, passionately and honestly in front of others. It is the fear which keeps you from doing those very things you most crave and desire to do and to accomplish. It is that feeling of fear which keeps you from caring too deeply for other human beings, for whatever reasons you may have about caring in this way of openness. It is that feeling of fear which keeps you from allowing yourself to be fully loved by another being, or to fearlessly love another when that is your heart's natural desire and impulse. It is that fear which keeps you in your secret loneliness, hiding and isolation. Need I go further with this explanation? Are you feeling this with me?

The evolutionary journey of feeling will, in time, bring you into contact with your inner wound. This evolutionary journey will bring you into feeling the deep fear down in your belly; deep down in the underworld domain of your primal humanness. When you come into authentic contact with this fear, this inner wound, deep down in your feeling underworld, it may arise as an emotional experience such as this...there is a sense of feeling very young, somewhat helpless and childlike. The inner wound in your humanness may be experienced as a feeling of innocence, weakness, or vulnerability. There may be a sense of fear, confusion, neediness, loneliness and deep feelings of lack and disconnection.

In this wound there is a strong and unconscious tendency to need and grasp for safety, security, warmth, love, connection and nurturing. There is a sense of desperately wanting to fill something up inside of you that feels empty, lacking and deficient. Hiding within the emotional domain of this inner wound, there may be feelings of being abandoned, rejected, betrayed, separated, cut off, unloved, uncared for, and a deep sense of being unworthy of love.

This inner wound is a portion of what you experience as your feelings, as your emotional self, as your deep and primal humanness. This inner wound is a large portion of your humanness, of your human psychology. And yet, much of who you have become, and how you have cleverly designed your personality, is based upon your unconscious avoidance, denial and rejection of this part of your being! Much of what you choose to do with your personal time and energy is actually based upon your unconscious attempts to avoid, hide and distract yourself from these deep, hidden feelings within you. And, most often, your need and grasping will move in unconscious ways

toward other people, food, drugs, material possessions and circum-
stances in the outer world, in an attempt to fill and satisfy this deep
sense of lack within yourself. This part of your primal humanness is
the most denied and disowned aspect of the human psyche. Does any
of this offering feel familiar to you?

If only you could know and feel how deeply I am pour-
ing out my heart to you, offering you the care, nurturing
and love you need and so desire. My life dances within
every cell of your being. I touch and feel your need, your
yearning, your every tear...with the deepest part of my
heart...if only you could feel...

...And this is the deep meaning and intention of all
of my words to you. On the evolutionary path of feeling
and awakening, you are only now just learning to feel.
You are only now just beginning to soften, open, receive
and surrender. The fear, the hardness, the separation
you have created within yourself and between one
another...all of this holds back the love and wisdom that
I am giving to you at all times. Your fear and hardness
blocks your inherent ability to feel and receive from me,
from others, from life itself. You are in the evolutionary
process of opening to True and Authentic Feeling...
opening yourself to Love's True Expression. You are
in the evolutionary process of softening, melting and
opening. You are entering the Heart's Domain of Sacred
Vulnerability and you are navigating the Newness of
Undefended Feeling.

I would like to welcome you with my entire heart into

the Living Presence of Love. I would like to welcome you into your resurrection of deep sensitivity, sacred vulnerability and undefended feeling...this is the opening of your heart and body. This evolutionary unfolding is how I express my dance of love within you. And here is an offering...*your inner wound is that part of Self which is now in the process of healing and coming into birth...that part of Self which is now deciding if it feels safe enough to open, blossom, feel and express...that part of Self which is only now beginning to receive the radiance of your awareness, acceptance and love.* Your inner wound is also a part of your child self, your sensitive feeling self, your inherent innocence, the part of Self who has been protected, armored, covered and kept away from the joyous light of fearless and innocent play. This child is learning to feel safe, learning to open and trust. This emotional child within you is also learning how not to hurt others when it is feeling hurt or when it wants its own way! For although this part of yourself has qualities and feelings like a young, innocent and vulnerable child, this part of yourself is also an integral part of your primal sexual and creative power! In the underworld emotional domain of your humanness, all of these aspects of your psyche are intricately connected and interwoven.

Let us go deeper into your body and into your humanness now. Come along with me if you will. Allow yourself to relax, soften and feel into your belly. Soften your heart as well and relax into your breathing. Let down the structured defenses and excuses of your rational mind.

Allow yourself to drop gently down into your body, into your fear, into your vulnerability. Experience, feel and look around from this within place...from the within of your softness, vulnerability and openness. Come along with me as I offer the following feelings to you as your own inner voice...as a voice from the inner wound...as a voice of your own humanness speaking to you from within. Come, read slowly, listen and feel with me...

"I am vulnerable and so afraid. Much of the time I feel fragile and much too delicate for this world. Or I just pretend to be strong and fearless so I can cope. I feel like I could easily be hurt or wounded. I feel as if I am wounded. I moan and whimper in fear, lack and need. I am afraid, I feel young, I do not want to grow, I am afraid to grow, I do not know how to grow. I need help. I am afraid to open and feel. I am feeling only fear. Nobody will love me. Nobody will ever love my ugliness, my woundedness. I feel like I am all alone. I want nurturing but I push others away. Maybe I am not worthy of love or nurturing. I am afraid to reach out. I am afraid to ask for what I want and need...I might be rejected, abandoned, or hurt. I don't trust anybody. I don't trust myself. I am afraid of my own power. I am afraid of my own desire. I fear the power of my desire. I need others, but I don't want to need anyone. I am afraid of my own needs, and even afraid of expressing my needs. If I express my needs I fear I will be rejected. If I express my power, desire and beauty, I fear I will cause harm to others or be rejected for my radiance. I will just stay small and weak. I feel lonely, angry, bitter and hurt. I want others to take care of me, to see me, to hear me, to validate me, recognize and understand me. I am angry at others for not feeling me, seeing me, understanding me and validating me. I am angry at myself for not feeling and seeing myself, for not understanding and validating myself. I do not know my way out of this, and maybe nobody will ever come to help me, save me, or show me the way out."

This voice is an example of the underneath place, the underworld domain of your emotional self. This is the voice of the inner wound. This is a voice expressing the deeply denied feelings from the primal and emotional humanness, feelings which all beings have and experience to some degree. This is a voice expressing that which has been pushed down, abandoned, rejected and disowned in the human psyche. This is the voice from the denied emotional self. This is the wound, the core sense of lack and separation from the cutting of the cord at birth. This is the buried feeling wound of self-perceived separation from Source. The feeling of separation and lack which continues even now because you yourself have been so deeply afraid to feel and embrace this denied and disowned part of yourself.

I offer you a key...a key of deep wisdom which has the power to unlock many psychological and spiritual mysteries...

...This part of yourself feels cut-off, separate, rejected, abandoned and wounded because of your personal and collective lack of acceptance toward it, because of your personal and collective unwillingness to feel into it and embrace it! This aspect of your psyche,

this part of yourself, is what human beings have judged, rejected, denied and disowned for ages. Is it any wonder this part of Self feels wounded, rejected, abandoned, unseen, unworthy of love and separated from Source?

So often you harshly and insensitively judge this soft and feeling part of yourself. So often do you unconsciously push this creative and powerful part of Self back down as it makes an attempt to rise, express and speak. In this way, as you judge and deny this aspect of your primal humanness, you push it even further into its fear and feelings of separation, rejection, abandonment and unworthiness. And in an attempt to compensate for the weakness you feel from this inner wound, you tend to move your actions into the world with a false and over-compensated sense of confidence, power, fearlessness and strength. To prove yourself worthy and to elevate yourself for esteem, trying so desperately to compensate for your inner feelings of fear and lack, you make so many goals in your life important. You choose goals and priorities for yourself which are not eternal and which will only turn to dust in short time.

Hear me and understand…your softened and loving heart must open to and lovingly embrace this deep human aspect of your psyche. For I ask you, who will connect with, accept, understand, nurture, love and care for this part of yourself, if not your own heart of loving acceptance? Who will finally offer this denied part of your humanness the opportunity to grow, mature and express, if not your own willing, accepting and guiding heart? Please take some time to consider what I offer here.

I continue now…in revealing a great mystery. Your very own heart and mind have come to fear this wounded, denied and disowned part of Self. Collectively, human beings have come to fear this aspect of the psyche. The reason being that so often, in your attempts to fill and satisfy your unconscious feelings of lack, neediness, unworthiness, loneliness and isolation, you have acted in ways of anger, control, manipulation, dishonesty, hostility and violence. Motivated by your desperate and unconscious hunger for love, security, nurturing and sexual/emotional fulfillment, you may act in hurtful, grasping, manipulative, controlling and dishonest ways toward others. *You act in these ways so as to get the love and attention that this denied and abandoned part of your primal humanness needs, wants and so desperately desires.* Your deep and feeling heart, your conscience, which knows better, does not want to be acting in these hurtful, dishonest, or desperate ways toward others. Yet you seem to have no ability to understand this unconscious behavior or the power to change it. To cope with this condition, you continue to judge and be fearful of this part of your wild and primal humanness. You continue to be afraid of how your humanness habitually misuses power; afraid of the hurtful ways in which you are capable of behaving when trying to satisfy your human needs and desires.

In this way of coping, you continue to push this part of your own humanness even further into fragmentation. You push this part of your humanness even further into separation, even further into feelings of unworthiness, loneliness, rejection, betrayal and abandonment. When you push away and deny this part of yourself, then your mind and body dissociate. This is what creates the splitting apart of your mind and your body. This is what creates the splitting apart of thought and feeling, of male and female within you, wherein these parts of Self are no longer in communion and harmony with one another. This unconscious condition, this psycho-emotional mystery has plagued humanity for ages.

Do you understand what I am bringing to you here? These words, this inner story of your own humanness comes to you from the deep underneath places. This inner story comes forth from the depths of your own being, where most of you are not yet conscious, from where most of you choose not to feel, navigate or explore with your awareness. On the evolutionary path of feeling, it is crucial that you willingly cultivate a *conscious feeling relationship* with this part of yourself, with this aspect of your own humanness. And yet, most often, you wait until you are unexpectedly and uncomfortably introduced to this denied part of yourself by way of difficult, deeply painful or tragic experiences in your life. I will offer that a deep part of your primal humanness is calling for your awareness...calling for your loving heart...awaiting and yearning for a more sensitive and conscious feeling relationship.

Please understand: that which you judge of yourself, that which you fear of yourself, that which you deny, reject and abandon of yourself, that is pushed away into unconscious domains of fragmentation and separation. And these parts of yourself feel this rejection, disowning and separation. All beings everywhere, and all parts of yourself, all aspects of your psyche, fully need and desire the Loving Acceptance of Heart. All beings everywhere, and all parts of yourself, fully desire and need the Loving Acceptance of Heart so as to have an entrance back into the Heart...which is the Origin of all things.

Although this inner wound, this sensitive, innocent, hurt and desperate part of your humanness frightens you, this part of yourself deeply needs and wants the full acceptance and understanding of your loving heart. This part of yourself needs the wise guidance of your heart. Can you sense and feel what I am offering to you? Listen to me with your whole body. You are the one who must be able to accept, understand and deeply care for this part of your own Self; this part of your humanness which feels so wounded, abandoned, betrayed and alone.

As you bring the loving acceptance and understanding of your heart to this disowned part of yourself, this aspect of your being will begin to trust, heal, transform, grow and blossom. As you allow this emotional/feeling aspect of your humanness to voice and express its needs, without fearing rejection, and without blaming or harming others when you do not get what you want, you give this part of your humanness the gift of creative expression. As you learn to love and nurture this part of yourself, you will naturally cease your desperate and unconscious grasping toward others, expecting them to give you exactly what you have been unwilling and unable to give yourself —love, connection, acceptance, validation and nurturing! In this way, there is more space for love, intimacy and tenderness in your relationships. As you offer your loving awareness and acceptance to this previously fragmented and disowned part of yourself, the war and conflict in your body, emotions and mind will come to a welcome end. This part of yourself will begin its integrative movement back into union and wholeness.

You yourself must make the choice to feel and embrace this rejected part of Self; this inner wound within you. On the journey of feeling and awakening, nothing must be left behind. You yourself are the one who must make the choice to cultivate a conscious feeling relationship with this part of Self, with all parts of Self. As you allow yourself to honestly and vulnerably embrace this inner wound without resistance, avoidance or denial, you will be able to move your feeling awareness directly into it. *This movement, connection and penetration of your feeling awareness, moving down into your humanness, this is the movement that delivers your light, your acceptance, your love and nurturing into this previously denied part of your being! This is an integral part of the evolutionary journey of feeling. This is the path of emotional maturity and awakening. This is the ongoing evolution of conscious embodiment. This is the process of descending into your humanness. This is your choice to cultivate a conscious feeling relationship with your own humanness. This is healing and*

*transformation. This is the ending of your denial, dissociation, frag-
mentation and separation. This is the beginning of integration,
wholeness and unity.*

Please consider...how could you possibly heal
and integrate this part of your psyche, if you are not
willing to feel into and open your heart to this part of
your humanness? You must be able and willing to accept,
embrace and feel this part of yourself so as to end the
separation and fragmentation created from your own
denial and avoidance. I offer this for your heart...*your
inner wound is your transformation. Going into your wound is
going into your transformation. Your inner wound is a part of your
feeling self...is an open doorway for entering true transformation.
Avoiding the feelings of the inner wound is simply a continuing
avoidance and denial of your own humanness.*

How do you feel now? Do these words carry enough
guidance for your journey in this moment? Take a breath.
Relax your mind into your body once again. For even
deeper clarity, let us continue further now. Why have
you so rejected this inner wound, this part of your primal humanness, and hidden it away in the underworld of
your being?

The inner wound, your own humanness, the emotional
self, holds within itself a very old and deep fear of loss.
The emotional self holds deep feelings of being abandoned, cut off and separated from Source, which is the
Heart. Your heart and your humanness, your body and
your mind, must reunite through openness, awareness and

loving acceptance. This self-perceived separation and wounding came into being as a part of your accepted journey into body and physicality, as part of your evolutionary journey into humanness.

This inner wound may also feel as if it was created from your physical mother as well, for it is she who gave birth to you. Much of the time, the birth process is violent, traumatic, and you were left with a deep feeling of being cut-off from your connection and nourishment. This is a deeply buried piece of memory stored in the unconscious domains of the primal humanness. Yet, I must offer this to you...*although it certainly may not feel as such, you have never truly been cut off. You were never cut off. Although it may be difficult for you to feel or imagine, based upon traumatic experiences early in your life, you have never truly been cut off, abandoned or been in separation. And yet, the significance of what I am offering here must surely await its validation and recognition until it naturally arises as your own direct experience. What I am offering here must await its validation and recognition until that time when it naturally arises as a revelation from your own explorations into deep feeling, and your complete and loving acceptance of your own primal humanness.*

You are the one who must make the choice to feel your way into the domain of the inner wound. You are the one who must enter into your emotional/feeling self; into the sacredness of your own humanness, to find what is true for you. You must be the courageous one who willingly enters into your own experiential discovery of integration and union. In this way of discovery, your sense of fragmentation and separation will give way to your ever-deepening awareness and experience of union. *Please understand, this inner wound, which is your emotional/feeling self, this is the child of heart. This child of your heart is the earth-based, human, psychological reflection of your larger Essence—your Heart, your Soul, your Spirit. This child of heart, your own primal humanness, must be welcomed back into your heart...since it is your own heart who is its Source, its Mother and Father. Your soul and your humanness, spirit and matter, are on an evolutionary journey into sacred union. This sacred union, this conscious feeling relationship, this evolutionary tantric embrace, must birth itself within the nurturing womb of your unconditional love and acceptance, free of judgment, resistance and denial.*

To deepen your understanding, I will continue this journey with a summary of what has been offered, yet with a different perspective; a different feeling presentation...

...This denied, rejected and abandoned part of Self, your inner feeling of separation, your deep fear of loss, this creates within you an outward moving and misguided grasping, desiring and attachment. *You grasp and reach outward into the world and toward others to find the connection, validation, safety, love and nurturing you so deeply desire. You seek outwardly to fulfill your inherent need and desire for union. Most often your outward seeking, grasping and attachment are motivated by the unconscious feelings and fears which you have rejected and abandoned. Most often, you will reach outward, grasp and attach yourself to others in misguided ways in your attempt to find love and connection…in your attempt to fulfill your own denied and unconscious needs.* This offering is the revealing of a mystery, an answer as to why many relationships in your life continue to bring you confusion, frustration and pain.

You hold so tightly to life, that life can barely flow through you. You hold tightly so as to fulfill your inner need for love, safety, comfort and security. Yet this holding and attachment is the last thing you would like to admit to yourselves or others. For this grasping, neediness and attachment creates an embarrassment for you. This behavior creates great challenges for you because you have not been able to understand or feel what this disowned part of yourself is truly needing and calling for. You have not fully understood your outward movement of grasping, needing, desiring and attachment. *Your primal humanness appears to be calling for a thousand unfulfilled desires which can be satisfied from the outer world. And yet the truth of the matter is that your humanness is calling loudly for connection, for union, for the loving acceptance of your own heart!*

Please understand the simplicity within the many words of this offering. If you are afraid to feel, afraid to go deep into your own fear and wounding, afraid to open deeply into your emotional/feeling self, you cannot fully experience life because you are blocked from your own inherent feeling ability. For although your inner wound may contain fear and hurt and other such buried emotions, there are still the precious gifts of deep feeling, empathy, sensitivity and relatedness inherent in this part of yourself! Deep, rich and harmonious relationships in life require a sharing and blending of this beautiful and sensitive part of yourself. If you deny and cut off this part of your own humanness in the belly, you deny and cut off a bridge of human connection which brings you into relationship, into empathy, feeling, sensitivity, intimacy and union with yourself and others.

As you begin to open, soften and reconnect with previously denied parts of yourself, there will be a heightened sensitivity. This enhanced sensitivity may not be comfortable at first. For as I have told you, this opening is new, vulnerable and less defended. The old emotional armor begins to melt and fall away. The Awakening Fires of Love and Feeling within you burn with the power of intimacy. Naturally, there will be more vulnerability, openness and sensitivity to life. Remember, this part of yourself has been covered and numbed with veils of protection, defense, fear and avoidance. Opening to feeling, entering into deeper intimacy with yourself and others will have its own natural progress and time of unfolding. Opening to feeling, entering into deeper intimacy with yourself and others requires a sincere desire to grow consciously, a willingness to enter the newness...the Newness of Undefended Feeling.

Why does this wondrous process of touching the inner wound and opening the heart and body to undefended feeling bring so much resistance, confusion, fear and pain with it for so many people? Why does opening into this part of Self usually require a life challenge, a tragedy, the violent shaking of a difficult relationship, an illness, pain or even death? Why is this part of Self so denied, so protected and well defended? I have offered much in answering these questions for your heart and mind. And yet now I will answer again, in a new way. I will answer from a new direction. I will answer from a completely new paradigm of intimacy and awakening. I have also used the expression *inner wound* until now, so as to introduce you to a part of your primal humanness that you feel and perceive to be wounded. I have used the expression *inner wound* until now, so as to bring you into a deep feeling and recognition of this part of yourself that you feel and perceive to be wounded, broken or hurt. And yet now I offer this for your feeling and consideration...

...With the emphasis of my heart shining into your awareness from the newness, I declare to you...*you are not wounded! You were never wounded! You are not broken! There is nothing wrong with you at all! I offer this mystery to you... revealed with love...you are not wounded, you are challenged. You are not wounded, you are simply challenged to embrace your fear of opening to love and your Sacred Vulnerability at the same time. You are challenged to embrace your fear of opening and your Sacred Vulnerability at the same time, rather than stopping and freezing the process of opening your heart and body at your very first feelings of fear. If you are in the habit of stopping or freezing your feelings of vulnerability and intimacy because of your fear of opening your heart and body, you may feel and perceive yourself to be wounded.*

However, this is not the truth. If you learn to embrace your fear and your vulnerability together, at the same time, you will enter the challenge of intimacy which awaits you. Please read this until you feel and understand what is being offered.

Once again, you are not wounded. You are not dysfunctional. You are not in any way broken or damaged. And yet you are indeed faced with an Evolutionary Challenge of the Heart. You are challenged to embrace your fear of opening and the Newness of Undefended Feeling at the same time, in the same breath, rather than trying to stay safe and isolated in your frozen fear, contraction, protection and psychological defense. *Sacred Vulnerability* and the *Newness of Undefended Feeling* are calling you. They are your larger Essence, your Heart and Soul. They are Love Itself calling you into a deeper and more tender union with your Heart, with your Body, and with Others. And yet your habitual fear and self-perceived wounding calls loudly for attention as well.

Having an inner wound is only your emotional perception. In reality, the emotional or sensory perception of being wounded is a *misperception!* Yet this deep inner sense of fear and woundedness cannot be denied, for indeed it has become a very real part of your primal humanness. Understand that Sacred Vulnerability, and your fear of opening into this grand new experience, exists together in the areas of your heart and your lower body. Your fear, protection and defense, and what you feel of yourself to be wounded, all of this psycho-emotional material veils the experience of Sacred Vulnerability. All of this covers and obscures the tender Newness of Undefended Feeling. Your fear, protection, defense and perceived wounding, deep in your belly and heart, this is your own earth-based primal humanness, your personality structure, your ego, your personal psychology...wrapped around your larger Essence, your Heart, your Soul, your True Self. Because of this close relationship between the two, in opening to your Sacred Vulnerability and the Newness of Undefended Feeling, it may, in the beginning stages, feel exactly like opening to your fear or wounding. These words offer a subtle yet profound visceral insight for those who can find this feeling in their body.

Feel and understand...*just because you may be feeling your fear or wounding while opening yourself into Sacred Vulnerability, into love and intimacy with another being, this does not mean you are truly wounded! There is a natural fear which arises upon entering the Newness of Undefended Feeling and Sacred Vulnerability of the Heart and Body. You are feeling this fear of opening because you are being challenged to pass into and through the narrow doorway of your human fears and perceived wounding and enter into the larger and more spacious domain of Love, of Sacred Vulnerability... which is your Essence...which is your very Heart. Opening and feeling into that which is your larger Essence is new and challenging for all human beings. It is only natural for there to be some fear in this evolutionary experience, as your humanness is stretching, expanding and exercising its previously limited and habitual psychological boundaries. Once again, your human level fear and psy-*

chological defense strategies veil, surround and obscure the domain of Sacred Vulnerability, your True Heart. Your evolutionary challenge is to learn to embrace, enter and pass through your fear...while entering the Fearless Heart of Love. This Fearless Heart of Love exists throughout your entire body.

Please read and feel this declaration of my heart. I want to repeat this once again...when you are choosing to open yourself with tenderness, in relationship with your own Heart and Soul, or in relationship with another being whom you love, and you feel fear, this arising of fear is not happening because you are wounded. Your experience of fear is natural, and is happening because you are being challenged to lovingly embrace your fear and perceived wounding within the same moment that you are also embracing your Sacred Vulnerability and the Newness of Undefended Feeling. Opening your heart and your body into Sacred Vulnerability and the Newness of Undefended Feeling is a new and evolutionary challenge. Opening your heart and your body into a new paradigm of unconditional love and intimacy is a new and evolutionary challenge.

In relationship with others, you may have fear that the painful experiences of your past will arise again. You fear these experiences will repeat themselves if you dare to let down your protective defenses, opening your heart and body in vulnerability with another being. In relationship, you may fear losing control, losing your personal power, or losing the person whom you love, adore and need.

You may fear rejection, betrayal or getting hurt in some way. These fears, although you may try to keep them stored safely away under the surface of your awareness, still affect the quality and intimacy of your relationships. If you fear the painful, haunting experiences of your past, how will you enter into authentic and undefended relationship now? Please ask yourself, "If I am always fearing the past, how will I open my heart and body into the Sacred Vulnerability and intimacy of the moment when the opportunity arrives?"

Could it be what you fear even more than the painful experiences of your past, is the possibility of opening into the fearless, vulnerable and Undefended Heart of Love? Could it be that human beings fear the exploration of the unfamiliar and uncharted territory of the Open, Undefended Heart and Body? Could it be that what you actually fear most is your opening into the absolutely raw and naked Newness of Undefended Feeling? Could it be that even the contraction of fear feels safer and more comfortable for your humanness than the experience of opening into Sacred Vulnerability? This opening of the heart and body is new. This is an evolutionary challenge for all human beings. Will you courageously enter the domain of Intimacy, Sacred Vulnerability and Undefended Feeling, totally naked, free of psychological protection and defense?

You are not actually wounded, and you never were. Yes, you have had painful and harsh experiences in the past which continue to evoke fear, yet this does not mean you are wounded. You can certainly stay frozen and contracted in the hurt and pain of your past and choose not to open, or you can make the choice to embrace a grand evolutionary challenge. The grand evolutionary challenge which calls and invites you is simply this...

...*In each and every moment, in each and every breath, in each and every relationship, you are challenged to embrace your fear and your Sacred Vulnerability...at the same time. You are challenged to enter and embrace your fear and the Newness of Undefended Feeling...at the same time, in the same breath. You are challenged to open your heart and body into a new domain of intimacy and love, and not be held back by habitual patterns of fear, contraction and defense.*

I offer this from my heart...I offer you *The Practice of Open Embrace.* The Practice of Open Embrace invites you to openly embrace the love of Source within your heart, and to openly embrace the feelings of your primal humanness as well. The Practice of Open Embrace invites you to openly embrace both the love and vulnerability of your heart and the feelings of fear in your humanness. The Practice of Open Embrace invites you into a divine tantric embrace, this embrace being the sacred union of soul and humanness. After a short time of practicing this open embrace, of entering and embracing your fear and feelings of woundedness with awareness and love, those feelings will begin to dissolve. The fearless heart of intimacy will reign. Your inner relationship and outer relationships will all reflect a greater intimacy. You are not wounded, yet you are challenged. You are challenged to enter the Domain of Heart, challenged to enter the Domain of Sacred Vulnerability, challenged to embrace and open into the Living Presence of Love...naked and undefended.

I am the warm, gentle and powerful love which continually pours into your being, melting the last frozen coverings of your fear and denial. My love gently pushes its way into the tender bruise of your perceived wounding. And let this be finally revealed...your self-perceived wounding was never actually a wound...yet was and is and will always be...your continual birthing, your opening and evolving into the Newness of Undefended Feeling...your opening into Sacred Vulnerability...your opening into the Living Presence of Love. Hear these words...*there never was a wound...only a shadowy place of humanness where love, wisdom and intimacy had not yet arrived.* Remember...the journey does not end, it only deepens.

The Heart of Relationship:
Dancing In the Fire of Mutuality

Many of you are coming together at this time to explore relationship, with a deep desire for new and more conscious ways of sharing, relating and loving. As you come together with one another, do so with this understanding...that the reasons for your coming together may be much deeper and mysterious than simply the initial feelings of desire, attraction and happiness which pull you toward union with one another. Be aware of coming together for a grander, wondrous, more vulnerable and more fear-filled breaking of heart—a breaking into Heart.

In addition to fulfilling your need for love, companionship, nurturing and pleasure, be aware of coming together to dance in the fire of mutual transformation.

For in reality, it is the need for deep intimacy within all of you that brings you together for sharing. *It is the mysterious and driving need for deep intimacy, for exploring Sacred Vulnerability, which brings you into relationship and which brings you directly into your fears of relating in an undefended way. The need for deep intimacy, the need for sharing Sacred Vulnerability and Undefended Feeling…this need brings you into relationship, into your deepest fear, into your transformation, and ultimately, into your Fearless Heart.*

Deep intimacy, Sacred Vulnerability and the Newness of Undefended Feeling are all one and the same. Sacred Vulnerability is a mysterious and attractive force. Sacred Vulnerability is my heart, it is my need within you, and it is seeking every opportunity to explore itself through the dance of love in conscious relationship. Your heart and your body are desiring greater awareness, greater opening and continuing evolution. Your opening heart may be seeking a partner for tender navigation and sharing of this grand opportunity.

Please feel what I am offering…many of you come together in relationship from the strong, impulsive and magnetic allure of your emotional and sexual desire for love, safety, comfort, nurturing and pleasure. These feelings are only a small part of a deeper calling. Let this understanding be in your awareness as well…there is an evolutionary need within your heart and body, desiring to explore the wondrous experience of Sacred Vulnerability. This evolutionary need can also be voicing its desire for deep intimacy from just underneath the feelings of your attraction and desire for one another. Your sensitive body and heart instinctually and intuitively knows who they want for sharing their healing and opening. Your body, your heart, the evolutionary need for deep intimacy, this innate intelligence within you knows and feels and senses. Even though this innate evolutionary need for deep intimacy and Sacred Vulnerability is surrounded by unconscious defense strategies, protection and your fears of loss, this part of your being is still very much alive, sensitive and instinctual in its choices for who it feels to come together with in relationship.

In relationship, if either of you, because of your fear, try to grasp, hold, or control one another, in even the smallest of ways, you will simply bring out and reimburse unconscious fears and defenses. Sacred Vulnerability, the true essence of the heart, wants to share and explore the wondrous realms of love...wants to dance in the fire of mutuality. Sacred Vulnerability does not want to be grasped, held to, pushed, pulled, manipulated or controlled. In relationship, when one or both of you are experiencing fear and defense, and this remains unconscious within you, then your sharing of deep intimacy, Sacred Vulnerability and Undefended Feeling will be delayed. The delay of deep intimacy happens when the natural current of love is distorted by fear and defense. And yet, if both of you are able to fully embrace this fear and defense with awareness, acceptance, harmlessness and love, mutually supporting one another, then even this experience becomes an integral part of your exploration of deep intimacy. This is your transformation and this is the heart's way of relationship.

I speak to those of you who are choosing to softly open, who are choosing to go fearlessly into the exploration of your Sacred Vulnerability with one another. I ask you to come together with heart. I ask you to come together and offer nurturing to one another for the furthering of your mutual birth and opening into love. Come together in gentleness, in harmlessness, free of attachment or grasping. Come together in mutual and loving support of each other's opening into the Newness of Undefended Feeling. This is the heart's way of relationship.

In these accelerated times, it is possible that you will make the choice to leave someone you care for; one who may be avoiding and denying their evolutionary opening into the heart of love. This person may be unconsciously engaged in the fear, anger, violence or blame which arise from their avoidance of heart. If you do not have the ability or desire to nurture this relationship into a more tender and understanding place, or, if there does not appear to be a mutual vision of heart to move toward, then you must feel and follow your heart's deepest guidance. If you choose to move on, fear not, each of you will survive without the other. And the breaking apart may, in time, bring even greater opening to both of your hearts.

When you are exploring relationship, and one or both

of you are fearful, angry, violent or blaming, this experience is a loud behavioral confession of avoidance. This experience is a loud and obvious confession of the avoidance of heart and of exploring Sacred Vulnerability. In this experience of avoidance, neither of you are choosing to soften your defenses and neither of you will drink the nectar from the cup of love and transformation. And the reason for this is that in your fear, anger, violence or blaming, you are not able to gestate and birth consciously into the vulnerable places of deep intimacy and Undefended Feeling. Neither of you, because of your unconscious avoidance, are able to support one another safely, gently or harmlessly into the wondrous experience of love and Sacred Vulnerability.

If you have felt your calling, your attraction, perhaps toward a being who offers a softened and understanding heart...then be in your truth, integrity, honesty and power and follow your calling and attraction. The awakening fire of the heart calls loudly at this time. Do not stay where there is fear, anger, blame or violence. Do not stay where there is no movement into the experience of Undefended Feeling and the Shared Heart of Love. Do not stay where there is not enough heart for deep nurturing, intimacy and opening, if this is what your heart desires to experience.

There is a loud evolutionary call going forth from my fiery and passionate heart. Heart wants to dance with heart. Heart wants to support and strengthen heart.

Heart wants to grow with heart. The Fearless Heart wants to awaken all hearts into the fearless expression of love. The Sacred Vulnerability within all beings wants to come together to touch and explore and learn of Itself... through the mutual dance of love.

You can always choose to an example of the open, fearless and loving heart...this is the greatest service. However, you will not be able to save or help those who only say they want to grow, who say they want to open their heart, yet with the louder confession of their actual behavior show they are not willing to open. You can be an example of the loving heart, yet you will not be able to save or help those who will not embrace their fear and denial and walk vulnerably into the Newness of Undefended Feeling. If you stay in a relationship where there is avoidance of heart, avoidance of feeling, avoidance of opening, this choice will be from your own fear and avoidance of heart as well. Please listen to and follow the deep calling of your heart.

I offer this to the courageous ones...I offer this to those who are intuitively choosing to follow the guidance of heart...who are willing to touch and feel the transforming fires of their Sacred Vulnerability...you must be born first. You are the ones who must be birthed first into the Living Presence of Love...into the direct experience of Undefended Feeling...into the Fearless Heart. In this way, you are the ones, present and supportive with your open and educated heart, who will then assist your fellow human beings in their upcoming birth when they are ready and the timing is right.

An Enduring Smile
of Kindness

I smile into your humanness with kindness. I warm your being with a tender smile of deep understanding. Can you experience yourself as my smile of kindness, in relation to your own humanness? Can you experience yourself as the gentle radiance of a tender smile, in relation to your humanness? My enduring smile of kindness, tenderness and deep understanding, radiating its life-giving warmth into your human experience, is exactly that which keeps your heart beating, which gives you life and helps you grow and evolve. The gentle radiance of my enduring smile is the actual catalyst of your transformation and awakening, the pulse, momentum and rhythm of your evolutionary development. Just as the silent yet powerful rays of the sun bring vital nourishment to all things living, I radiate my enduring smile of kindness into your humanness. This is my offering of nourish-ment. This is the Living Presence of Love flowing into your human experience.

Are you harsh with yourself? Are you demanding and critical of yourself? Do you push your humanness, your body, forcing it to meet with your never-ending ideals, expectations and desired goals? Do you sense that your humanness, your body, will learn, grow and trans-form with this type of treatment? Do you feel that the harshness, demands or criticism of your impatient mind, unleashed upon your humanness, will actually assist your transformation or help you achieve your desired goals in life?

This is most certainly what the mind thinks! This is most certainly what the idealistic, perfection-oriented, demanding and impatient mind thinks. The mind, not infused with the wise and gentle understanding of the heart, thinks it can criticize, demand and push the humanness into transformation. The mind believes that by its constant onslaught of harshness it can transform stubborn behavioral patterns in the humanness and push the body toward achieving great goals. Please feel and understand, this is simply ego-based habitual con-ditioning trying to transform habitual conditioning. This behavior is the ego trying to transform itself. This approach is always doomed to futility and failure.

From the within of your heart and body, can you sense, feel, or intuit the supportive and life-giving radiance of my smile upon your humanness? From the silence, behind your personality, I smile upon and into your humanness with kindness, with tenderness. My enduring smile of kindness radiates from a deep understanding of your journey of awakening, and its natural evolutionary timing and unfoldment. Your harsh or critical treatment of yourself comes directly from your lack of understanding and impatience with your evolutionary journey in life. My enduring smile comes from the patience of the knowing and feeling heart. Can you relax your deep impatience and experience yourself as my smile of kindness in relation to your own humanness? Can you soften your heart, your body, and slow your mind enough so as to experience yourself as the one smiling this enduring kindness into your own humanness? The radiance of my smile is just underneath the surface of the restless, impatient mind and emotions.

Here is a mystery revealed. You are the one who unleashes the harshness upon your innocent humanness. And you are also the one who can choose to align with the loving heart and offer a warm smile of kindness into your humanness as well. *Your choice to offer this smile requires a shift of feeling perception—a shift from ego-based impatience and harshness to the kindness of the heart. Kindness is not an emotion or sentiment, it is the very nature and radiance of your Essence, the Heart. My enduring smile of kindness is the Natural Radiance of Heart. The Heart is my smile. My smile is your own True Heart, and kindness is the Essence of the Heart.*

Only the heart can offer the qualities that nourish and nurture transformation and awakening. The harshness of the critical, impatient mind cannot accomplish this. The harsh, critical and impatient mind can only bring more stress, more pain and more feeling of betrayal and separation into your humanness. The harsh and critical mind creates betrayal and separation because of its limited and dualistic perception...splitting apart mind and body, thought and feeling, the inner and the outer, the conscious and unconscious. The harsh, critical and impatient mind has not been touched by the tenderness, unity and deep understanding of the heart. *The understanding heart knows and feels the processes, rhythms and right timing of psychological and spiritual unfoldment. The impatient mind does not have access to this understanding or kindness...because it does not feel! It is only the heart that can feel.*

Can you sense how a gentle smile of kindness from the heart may have the actual power to nourish and nurture your humanness...nourish and nurture your transformation and awakening? Can you sense how an entire universe of love can express itself through a simple smile such as this? Can you sense how the harsh, impatient and critical mind has no true power to accomplish anything except more betrayal, separation and suffering... unless it is finally unified with the loving heart? Can you experience yourself as my enduring smile of kindness nourishing and supporting your own humanness? Can you experience yourself as the gentle radiance of a tender smile nurturing your humanness? This enduring smile of kindness is a nourishing, moist downpour of rain, entering into the dry, parched and waiting earth of your human experience. This enduring smile of kindness is the milk of the mother for her child. This enduring smile of kindness is the gentle, radiant glow of moonlight shining on your path at night. A smile of kindness bestows the life-giving warmth of the True Heart.

A simple smile of kindness is not just a nice thought, an emotion, a sentiment or a philosophical concept. An enduring smile of kindness requires a conscious choice... a choice to open your heart and offer this smile, through the radiance of feeling awareness, into your entire bodily experience. A smile of kindness is the choice to open the floodgates of your heart and mind, and smile your loving acceptance into your body...into your human experience. A smile of kindness is an actual and literal transmission of life-force radiating from the heart. A smile of kindness is a gift from the open heart...bringing nourishment and nurturing to the harshly treated and denied aspects of your humanness. A smile of kindness and loving acceptance from the heart...brings the harshly treated and denied aspects of your humanness out of separation and into wholeness, unity and integration.

I offer an enduring smile into your humanness with kindness. I smile into your human experience with the tenderness of deep understanding. Will you soften your heart and choose to smile with me? Will you feel, realize and experience...that you are my smile?

Honoring and Embracing
Your Moment

What does honoring and embracing your moment mean? In reality, in this very moment, the timelessness of heart is all you will ever have. This very moment is surely your opportunity to feel, grow and be fully intimate with yourself and others. The moment is the unfolding presence of who you are, in that exact moment of your experience. Each timeless moment of heart offers an opportunity for your passionate honesty and fearless expression of Self. Each moment in your experience is truly an opportunity of heart.

In any given moment, when you are feeling something, no matter what this feeling may be, learn to honor and embrace your feeling experience in that moment. Learn to honor and embrace your moment. If you do not choose to honor and embrace your moment, you are avoiding the aspect of Self which is arising in that moment of your feeling experience. If you are feeling something which you are uncomfortable with, and you are trying to avoid, resist, cover, or hide from this feeling in any way, you are not honoring and embracing the authenticity of your moment, or the aspect of Self which is arising in that moment.

In the exact moment you choose avoidance of feeling, it is in that moment you contract the heart, dishonor Self, stop your growth, and you stop the emerging expression of your feeling self. This is a fear of intimacy with your feeling self. Understand and feel, these dishonored and un-embraced moments collect and gather inside of your being. *Each time you avoid feeling, this avoidance weakens the fiery and passionate expression of heart and body. Your avoidance of feeling builds up until you are living in an isolated, fearful, lonely and false image of yourself...more out of touch with your feeling self...more out of touch with heart. Each time you avoid feeling, this resistance gets pushed deeper into the body, and you continue weakening your inherent feeling ability, rather than passionately allowing your feeling ability to emerge, express and grow.*

All of your avoided and denied moments gather, and will need your attention and loving acceptance at another time. These avoided moments will need to continue their emerging and growing process at the exact place where they were first avoided, denied, and disowned. These avoided moments of your feeling experience will need your attention by way of your willingness to feel them at some point in your journey. These avoided moments will need to be met and embraced with your willingness to be intimate with your feeling experience.

I offer this…in the exact moment you change or stop your natural expression of Self, because of fear or self-judgment, you are in avoidance of your feeling experience in that moment. This is limitation. Freedom and passion are born out of your ability to freely express your Self in any given moment without fear or self-judgment. If you resist, deny or avoid your humanness, deny or avoid your feeling self in any moment, then your humanness is not accepted by heart and cannot grow and evolve. If you accept, embrace and love your humanness, your humanness will blossom, grow and evolve as you continue allowing and accepting its emergence and expression in each moment.

This does not mean you will be wildly out of control if you allow your humanness or feeling self to freely and spontaneously express and grow. It simply means allowing your feeling experience to emerge without judgment or denial. Even what you consider to be the most terrible, fearful, selfish, angry or violent feelings can be honored and embraced. All of these feelings can be welcomed into the open, intimate and loving acceptance of your heart, without you having to act out any of these feelings toward yourself or others. *Opening to, accepting and honoring all of your feelings, no matter what they may be, does not mean you have to allow your feelings to influence your thoughts, speech or actions in a negative way. In fact, if you are able to open and soften your heart in loving acceptance to your feelings of fear, sadness, grief, pain, hurt, anger or violence, you will have much less tendency to express those feelings in distorted or harmful ways toward yourself or others. This is because those feelings are finally receiving the attention and loving acceptance they are needing and calling for! And when you can be accepting and intimate with your own feelings and needs in this way, then you will also have the ability to be accepting and intimate with the feelings and needs of others.*

If you allow the emergence and expression of feeling in any moment, your feeling self can express and will grow. Your life-force will move and dance through you. Your feeling self, your emotional self, your humanness, will surely need the wise and loving guidance of heart… yet your humanness will learn and evolve if you are able to honor and embrace your moment. If you honor and embrace your moment with honesty, passion and vulner-ability, you will allow all aspects of Self to grow from that moment…growing into the next…and into the next. And in one of these moments of timelessness, you will find that you have lovingly birthed the Fearless and Passionate Presence of Heart.

Waves, Clouds
and Burning Twigs

   If you are always struggling so as to stay afloat on the surface of the water, will you ever be able to feel and realize that you are the deep ocean itself? If you engage yourself with and indulge in every passing emotional wave, will you ever feel and realize that you are the larger ocean which gives birth to these ever passing waves? If your attention is fixed on every passing cloud in the sky, will you ever feel and realize that you are the clear and spacious sky itself, unaffected and undisturbed by the clouds which pass and disappear? If you feel yourself to be like a little twig burning in a large fire, will you ever feel and realize that you are indeed the burning fire itself, not the little twigs which burn into ashes? You are not the hurt, the pain, the guilt, the sorrow, the sins...you are the Living Presence of Love which embraces, heals, understands and forgives them all.

So long have you been deceived by the earthly quakes, winds, waves and fires of your life experience. And so long have you remained unaware of your Essence, unaware of your Awakening Heart, unaware of the Living Presence of Love within you. You are the Ocean of Being, not the ever-passing waves which continually appear and disappear. Your Essence is the clear, spacious sky of pure awareness, not the ever-changing clouds which come and go each day. You are the Living Fire of Love, not the little twigs of ego which get burned into ashes and are blown away by the winds.

And yet, from my heart I tell you, these words do not have the power to bring you into your Essence, into your Heart and Soul, into the Living Presence of Love. Only you have the power to desire and create this sacred and evolutionary experience. These words may soothe your being for a short time, yet they cannot give you the gift of heart that you are. These words may ignite a spark of remembrance in your heart for an instant, yet you must nurture this spark and bring it into expression as the Living Fire of Love. These words cannot awaken that which is already awake. These words can only speak to the forgetfulness which veils and dims your awakened and radiant heart. If your forgetfulness can listen, hear and feel for a moment, it becomes still. And in this stillness, the radiance of the heart can shine through into your forgetfulness, the fire can become brighter, remembrance comes to heart.

I can only remind you. I can only touch your heart with my whispers of love. I can only remind you of your soul's destiny with my songs from the within. It is your journey. You must feel and know your way back into union. You must learn to love your way back into remembrance of Source. You must learn to love and serve others unconditionally, knowing they are Self as well. This loving service, this feeling of unity, brings your awareness back into union with Source. Is there another way?

If you listen to all of the many whispers and shouts of the world, chasing and grasping at all of the hopes and dreams you believe will bring you happiness, you will surely pass from one thing to the next, experiencing only temporary satisfaction and much frustration. I offer you whispers of love and songs of awakening to touch and nurture the heart. I sing to you, reminding you of Self, of the Awakening Fire, of Source within you. There is no further to look, no further to feel, no further to search, than simply feeling and knowing the Intimate Stillness of the Heart as your own Center, as your truest Self, as Source. Breath, relax into your body and know Self. Breath, relax into your body and feel Self. Begin by relaxing into what you are feeling in this very moment. Then go to the next moment and the next, from truth to truth as truth unfolds for you. Relax into Source, into your own body and into the stillness and peace of the

Heart. This is the unfoldment, this is the journey, this is the invitation.

Seek far and wide for what you will, all beings come back home in their own time. And home is always where heart is. Heart is always ready to welcome you home. Come back, come back, come back to the Intimate Stillness, Peace and Tenderness of the Heart. Come back to the stillness within the center of your own being. Just breathe...just breathe, just feel and love as each moment unfolds itself into the next. What is really important in life? Are you moving too fast to know and feel? Do you have so many cherished goals to accomplish in the future that you do not feel and recognize what is of true significance in this moment? Will disappointment, frustration, pain or hardship be my entrance into your heart? Or will you consciously choose to soften, open and feel before those challenging life experiences arrive as my messenger? I know you can feel my voice speaking to you from the within of your being. I know you are hearing my song. It is time...it is time. The invitation has been offered. Breathe, relax, let go of the external, come home. Breathe and feel and come back to your heart. Become still and silent and know your own Self, your own Soul, your own Heart...welcome home.

The Choice
and the Gift

For just a moment, I would like you to clearly imagine and deeply feel yourself letting go of every single thing you hope for in this life. Clearly imagine and deeply feel yourself surrendering, letting go and giving up everyone and everything you most cherish and desire. As you are imagining and feeling this surrendering, this letting go and giving up...I ask you this question...what will remain of you; who will remain? If you surrender your fearful holding and grasping, if you let go of your most cherished concepts and your deepest emotional attachments, what will remain of you? Do you dare find out? Do you dare feel into and explore this place of awareness?

Most beings will not dare, will not pursue or even

consider this experience. For this experience of release is as greatly feared as is the actual experience of death itself. And yet, at the end of one's physical life, what is the actual experience of death about? Certainly the experience of physical death is but a letting go; a releasing of so much that you have known and held to in the earthly domain. If only you knew…if only you could feel deeply into the underneath places of your awareness…you might discover that what you unknowingly desire and crave most of all…is a death!

The great death you unknowingly desire and long for…is the death of your fearful, contracted holding, grasping and possessing; the death of your fear-filled emotional attachments. The great death you unknowingly desire and long for…is the death of your false perceptions and concepts of reality, the death of your inner conflict, the death of your unconscious resistance to life. This is the death which has the power to dissolve the deep tension and conflict within your body, mind and heart. This is the death which brings a flood of life's love, wisdom, joy and radiance into your being. This death is actually life itself in thin disguise.

The world has endless offerings for your desires. You enjoy satisfying your physical, emotional, mental and spiritual desires in one way or another. When your desires are satisfied, you feel happy or content for a short while, until of course, the next desire arises! And this cycle of desire goes on and on continually, does it not? Please understand, desire itself is not your enemy. Surely desire has its own inherent wisdom and is a portion of my life movement within you. Yet what is it within you that motivates and pushes your desire continually outward into the world for satisfaction and fulfillment? What is it you are reaching to find in this external fulfillment of your desire? And what might it be that you are moving away from within yourself? When does this continual cycle of outward moving desire end? These are deep and valuable questions I offer for your consideration.

This cycle of desire, grasping and attachment can be slowed down. It can come to a relaxed and welcome end, when you finally feel and directly experience...the Gift. Yes, I have a Gift to offer...a Gift which brings the happiness and fulfillment you so desire and seek. And the fulfillment experienced from receiving this Gift will not be temporary...will not fade away as do the momentary pleasures you gain from your never-ending worldly desires. Yet how can I bring this Gift to you? How can I sing just the right song into your heart or speak just the right and revealing words to your mind? How can I bring you into just the right experiences so you can openly perceive, feel and receive this Gift? I have spoken to you and have presented myself to you through the art, the drama, the poetry, the songs of love and the holy scriptures for ages now. What is left? How can I show you...how can I awaken you? I can only help awaken you if you will listen, feel, if you will make the choice to receive my Gift. Is it your time?

Deep within your heart you will feel and know if it is your time. If it is your time, you must be the one who makes the choice... the choice to receive the Gift. To receive this Gift with open hands and heart and mind, you must first be willing to release your tightened grasp upon the outer world around you so that your hands and heart and mind are free to receive! As you release and retrieve your endless desire and take your attention back from the outer world, you can then use that same desire and attention to practice consciously relaxing into the Peaceful Stillness of the Heart. Desiring the Peaceful Stillness of the Heart must be your own choice, must be a movement of your own will. And surely it is in the direct experience of this Peaceful Stillness of Heart that you will begin to awaken. It is within the direct personal experience of this peaceful and still center of your being that you will learn how to harmoniously blend your awakening with the activities and responsibilities of your daily life. And surely it is within the direct bodily experience of this Peaceful Stillness of your Heart that you will receive the Gift...the Gift of Life.

This Gift of Life, found within the Peaceful Stillness of the Heart, offers the substance of true satisfaction and fulfillment. This Gift has the power to finally slow down your continually outward-moving desire for temporary and inferior forms of satisfaction and fulfillment. This Gift of Life, this substance of true satisfaction and fulfillment in the heart, gives you exactly that which you were so desperately and unconsciously trying to find in the external fulfillment of your endless desires. This Gift of Life has the power to fill and nurture the deep feelings of need, lack and loneliness within you, and will gradually dissolve the tendency to run away from these previously feared and denied feelings. Receiving this Gift of Life, this nourishing substance of true satisfaction and fulfillment, is the only true and lasting way to end the continual cycle of unconscious, outward-moving desire and grasping.

Please know and feel this mystery...I have already given you my Gift. I have already given you my Gift... for I am your Gift. I am your Life. I am your passion and I am the burning fire in your beating heart. You use me. You use my life energy. You use my fire. You use my love and my passion for each and every one of your desires, for each and every one of your impulses and cravings. Even the temporary satisfaction you experience after fulfilling your desire is simply the experience of my life energy as well. All of this is the Gift of Life...the Essential Self within your heart. All of this is mine. The desire is mine. That which is desired is mine, and the happiness you experience from the fulfillment of your desire is mine. All of this is, and originates from, the Gift of Life, the Presence of Source within your own heart.

And yet you are still in the evolutionary process of getting to know me and realizing the Gift within you. You are still cultivating your relationship and union with the Heart...with Source...with the Gift of Life within you. *Most often, you do not feel, sense or see me because your awareness, your mind, your will, your attention, your intention, your emotional desire...is always moving outward into the external world! Your attention and desire is always moving outward toward something you apparently need, want and crave. When your mind, your will and your desire are constantly moving outward, it becomes very difficult for you to feel and perceive the Gift of Life within you.* Once again, this Gift of Life within you is exactly that same vitality, energy and force you use to move your desire and craving outward in your frantic search for happiness and satisfaction! Your personal vitality, life-force and desire are only made possible because of the vital Gift of Life which is beating inside of your own heart! Desire can be your obstacle and your blindness, or desire can become your awakening. This all depends upon how you choose to direct and guide the movement of your desire. This choice is for you to consider.

This Gift I offer to you is not wrapped in a colorful, decorated package. This Gift is not meant to impress you or capture your attention. For in reality, this Gift of Life is already your attention! The Gift of Life within you *is* your attention and awareness. This Gift is always and openly offered, yet is mysteriously hidden in a very amazing and secure place. This Gift is hidden, yet it is completely available. This Gift of Life is available just underneath, just in back of, all of your outward movements and motions. It is available just underneath all of your fears, emotional attachments, and your many desires for all those things which you feel will bring happiness and fulfillment.

It is my deepest passion that you should find and feel

and know my Gift. Yet how can I touch you with this Reality? How can I convince you of its presence and priceless nature? I cannot convince you. I cannot lead your attention and awareness where you do not choose to go. I can only continue to call you with my songs of awakening. I can only sing to you from the within of your heart. Yet my songs rarely reach or touch minds and hearts given to the cares and endless desires of the material world.

So I ask you...can you take just a little time to relax? Can you practice dying before your actual physical death and learn to relax into the Peaceful Stillness of your Heart? Can you...will you...turn the outward movement of your mind, awareness and feelings around? Can you...will you...bring your attention away from the cares of the world and back into the Center of your own Being? In this way, we can meet. In this way, we can touch. In this way, we can share just a moment of timelessness together. In this way, we could get to know and feel one another...passionately and intimately from within the depths of the heart's stillness, silence and peace. In this way, I could offer you my Gift.

I have asked, I have offered my Gift. It is yours to answer. It is yours to receive. My Gift has always been and will always be yours. I love you always from the within of your heart. I sing to you always from the within of your heart. I am the one who sings the Gift of Life and Vitality into your blood and into your desire.

This Gift of Life, this Vitality of Source, my life within you, this is the vital energy you use to move outward through your heart and mind and bodily senses into endless desires, pursuits and goals. This outward movement of yours is not wrong or bad, it is simply your evolutionary exploration of being human. Yet I would suggest that to meet me, to feel me and to come into deeper communion with me, you will need to cultivate the practice of slowing down your outward moving pace. I am not asking you to renounce or deny your desires. I am not asking you to renounce or turn your back on the world, your loved ones, or your responsibilities. I am only asking that you also give some time and attention to your heart...some time and dedicated attention to relaxing into the Peaceful Stillness of the Heart. You can practice this while you work. You can practice this while you are walking. You can practice this through your prayer or meditation. You can do this simple practice of relaxing into the Peaceful Stillness of the Heart at any time and in any place. It is a choice. It is your choice.

You must open the eyes of your heart to see me, feel me and know me. You must relax into your body and into the stillness of the heart to feel me and commune with me. After you have given some time to this practice...after you have given some time to feeling, absorbing and assimilating my Gift of Life within you, then you will meet me everywhere you go. There is no mystery for the opened heart. Then you will see me in every being you encounter. There is no mystery for the awakened heart. Then you will feel me in everyone and in everything. There is no mystery for the feeling heart. And ultimately, there is no direction of outward or inward, no direction of up or down within the open spaciousness of the Awakened Heart. Yet this awareness, this realization, this awakening, this direct experience of your True Self, this receiving of my Gift of Life, this does indeed take some dedication and cultivation. Your attention must be turned around and brought back into the Peaceful Stillness of your Heart so as to directly experience and receive the Gift of Life.

The choice is yours to consider. I have asked, it is yours to answer. Your choice is your answer. The movement and direction of your will, desire and attention is your answer. Your actions are the loud and living confession of your answer and your choice. My Gift has always been available to you and will always be yours. I love you always from the within of your heart. I sing my songs to you with passion and love, will you listen? I sing to you always. I love you always from the within of our One Heart...listen...feel...be aware.

The Dance of Your Heart's Deepest Desire

I come to be with you at this time with a slightly different mood and voice of my feeling. Will you invite me in to be with you? Will you allow your awareness and feeling to be with me? If your answer is yes, even from the deepest parts of your being, then in your opening and awakening you will lose what you call control. In your softening, opening, receptivity and awakening, you will lose much of what you have thought and felt yourself to be. In your opening and awakening, you will surely be letting go of and dying to one part of yourself while you are awakening into the new life of a larger part. And this process, your opening, receptivity and awakening, will unfold as the blossoming of the most beautiful lotus flower.

In the wondrous unfolding process of your opening and awakening, at times you may cry, mourn or grieve. At times you may dance wildly with joy. In this unfolding, there may be times you feel confused, sad, lonely, depressed, angry or irritable. At times you may feel lost without direction. You may also experience the joy and radiance of awakening infusing your entire being. And when you have laughed and cried, moaned, groaned and labored, crawled through the depths and soared through the heights of the many unfolding layers of your own birthing...finally...you will stand alone, passionate, wild and awake!

What will you do now...alone, passionate, wild and awake? Surely you will do exactly that which your heart desires to express in each spontaneous moment of your awakened unfolding. *And you can rest in sureness that your offerings to other beings will be given from your awakened understanding of love, from your deep commitment to truth, and from your sincere compassion for your fellow beings. Sincere compassion for your fellow beings arises naturally as your awakened heart senses that their unconscious, misguided and desperate struggle is always grasping for that very same Essence which is now pulsing alive and awake within you. Your fellow beings unknowingly crave and seek that very same Essence which now looks out from behind your eyes... for they are not as yet feeling or knowing this radiant Essence as their own True Self. Essence...the Living Presence of Love, is always moved into sincere compassion when encountering Itself in other beings who are still in the process of struggling and awakening.*

Those who can hear, please hear and sense what I offer. Those whose hearts can feel, please feel and experience what I offer here...

...In the times of your opening, receptivity and awakening, you will be guided by my pulse. You will be guided by the pulse and rhythm of a New Understanding of Love. You will be guided by a silent voice of knowing within you. You will be guided by the sure pulse, rhythm and creation of a New World of Heart...opening itself up within the old world... in unfolding moments of timelessness. With this new pulse, this new rhythm, this new love alive in your being... you will surely be guided more by your heartfelt desire to feed and to nourish others, rather than by a need to feed and nourish yourself. In the times of your opening and awakening, your body will be guided and moved by my wise and loving pulse and rhythm. And this, our deep, mutual and intimate union, will surely be the dance of your heart's deepest desire.

In the times of your blossoming and awakening...all experiences, perceptions and feelings, of your own and others, will stand revealed and transparent to your tender and sensitive heart and body. With an undefended and awakening heart, all experiences and perceptions will be new. You will see and feel with new eyes and a new heart. *With this sensitivity of heart, you may find your life to be wondrous, and, at the same time, you may also experience some confusion or fear. For now your newly opening and tender heart walks in a world where people do not always recognize this beauty, nor do they speak the language or sing the songs your heart now feels. At times you walk alone. At times you share the beauty of the heart with other souls. These challenging yet fertile experiences of aloneness will greatly encourage the deep maturing of your heart! These challenging yet fertile experiences will greatly encourage the steadiness and poise of your feeling self, the blossoming of your wisdom and self-mastery, and your deeper understanding of serving humanity with a selfless love. Please hear me...the times of your opening, receptivity and awakening will require the virtues of acceptance, patience and deep compassion for self and others.*

If you invite me in to be with you, rest in sureness, you will lose much. If you invite me in to be with you, and you allow your awareness to come into union with me, rest in sureness, you will gain much. The choice is always yours...will you have me? I offer this from my heart, in deep love to you...*holiness, wholeness, is alive and available within your very being. Sacredness is who you are. Do not search far for these qualities. Be silent, be still and be quiet enough to feel and realize these innate qualities from the deep within of your being. In the Peaceful Stillness of the Heart, be aware and awake. In this Peaceful Stillness of Heart, holiness and sacredness blossom naturally from within your being...revealed as your very Essence.*

The Way of the Undefended and Receptive Heart

In times to come, much will be shifting and changing within your body, within your heart and within your mind. There will be much renewal and transformation of those old ways of being which no longer nurture and support your newly opening heart and the deepening of your feeling. What song of awakening may I offer you? What living words of love can I give so as to prepare you for this ever-unfolding journey into feeling...into the heart of openness?

Prepare yourself in this way...

Learn to relax your awareness down into your heart and into your body. Relax your awareness into your breathing. Enter and become one with your breathing, free of restless thought or emotion...this is an excellent practice. Willingly release your grasp upon the outer world. Willingly release your grasp upon even those whom you love and care for. Can you feel this offering? Although it may feel frightening at first, this letting go and releasing will change the direction and flow of your awareness and your desire. Although this practice may not come easily at first, this release of grasping and shift of your attention will naturally bring you back into your own Center of Being. Turning the direction of your awareness and desire around will naturally bring you deeper into the Peaceful Stillness of your own Heart. If you give this new learning some time and nurturing, this letting go and releasing of your grasp will deliver you into the destination you were unconsciously seeking and desiring.

As you touch the Center, the very Essence of your being, the Heart, you will begin to understand that this same Essence is exactly what you were unconsciously grasping for in others, in possessions, in food and in the circumstances of your outer life! There is only One Essence...One Heart...One Self. And this One Essence lives within the heart of all beings. *Upon the journey of your awakening, you will finally and ultimately feel and realize there is nothing in the world, or in the entire infinite universe, that you need hold to or grasp for. You already exist as that very Essence for which you would grasp. That Essence, for which you would grasp, already exists as you...as the very Essence of your own Being. And this Essence is alive and well...in the Center of your own Heart!*

As you cultivate a deeper feeling-union with your Essence, the Heart, you will naturally and effortlessly loosen your holding, grasping, controlling and possessing. In a very natural way, you will find yourself not holding so tightly or grasping so desperately at others, at your own thoughts and feelings, and at those things outside of yourself. As you cultivate a deeper feeling-union with your Essence, the Heart, you will know and feel that none of these objects of impermanence can ever provide you with the lasting love and security you are so deeply wanting. Love and security come only from the Essence within you...the Living Presence of Source within your very Heart. With this understanding and experience, your mind, body and heart will naturally let go of their anxiety and deepen into more relaxation. In deeper relaxation, your mind, body and heart will come alive and be capable of even greater intimacy with others and with life.

Grasping creates a tension, tightness and contraction in your body. This fear-based motion of grasping holds back the expression of True Intimacy. Holding so tightly to life and to others leaves room for only the self-centered desires you so desperately wish to grasp, extract and hold onto. There is little space left for anything else. All holding and grasping is a nonverbal, yet obvious behavioral confession of your fear of loss. All holding and grasping is a loud behavioral confession of an undeveloped relationship with your True Self... with Source...with the very Essence and Heart of your Being.

When you release your fearful holding and grasping, I can be with you in a new way. When you release, breathe and relax, your expansion and spaciousness becomes my entrance into your being. When you grasp, this behavior is an obvious confession of your fear of loss. Grasping is a confession of your unconscious feelings of lack and sense of separation from Source. In your grasping, you are reaching only for imagined needs and desires, which mysteriously distance themselves as your fearful grasp tightens. *When you release your fearful grasping and bring your attention and desire back into your own Center, then your mind, body and heart will naturally relax, open and become more peaceful. This cultivation, this practice, allows more space for your Essence to enter and assimilate into your humanness...allows more space for true intimacy and love to birth within you. And surely...it is this intimacy and love that you have been so deeply desiring and grasping for.*

If you continue in your habitual and fearful ways of grasping, holding and controlling, your experiences in life are certain to be those of constant challenge, frustration, unhappiness or pain. At some point in your journey, after these challenging life experiences have offered their supreme service of wearing down your argument with Reality, you will finally understand the ultimate futility of living your life in this way of fear and control. You can receive the love and wisdom of the heart and learn your necessary life lessons through struggle, frustration and pain, or you can receive these gifts of the heart in more conscious, direct, peaceful and harmonious ways. It is certainly up to you.

The love and wisdom of the heart, which are your necessary life lessons, these are the songs I sing to guide you on your path of awakening. My voice, my guidance, my love and wisdom…can come into you, can touch and teach you…only in those places of heart you make soft, open and receptive. When you move into your grasping or controlling in life, my guiding songs of love and wisdom are not easily felt, received or understood from within your fearful, contracted heart and body. And if not through the entrance of your undefended, receptive and listening heart, then how will life offer you its love and wisdom?

The fearful and contracted heart does not easily learn its necessary life-lessons from within or from its daily experiences, because it cannot feel or perceive Reality correctly. Constant struggle, confusion, frustration and pain naturally arise from this argument with Reality. The Undefended and Receptive Heart willingly listens, hears, feels and more easily receives my guidance…the love and wisdom of life's lessons. The Undefended and Receptive Heart can sense, feel and perceive Reality more clearly and accurately because of its openness. In this way, free of an argument with Reality, all relationships and events in life, no matter how they turn out, can always be experienced as welcome messengers of the heart's love and wisdom. I offer this so as to guide you into a new way of being…a new way of learning…a new way of listening…a new way of growing and loving…the Way of the Undefended and Receptive Heart.

Again, I offer this for your preparation...

Each and every day, take a little time to breathe and relax. Each and every day, practice softening and releasing your fearful holding, grasping and controlling. Learn to loosen your fear-based grasp on life. Ultimately, you will lose nothing...and ultimately, you will find your True Self...your Heart...the very Essence of your Being. And in this finding of your Heart, you will be able to share this priceless gift with the entire world. You will share the gifts of your heart with others in ways of effortless openness and deepening beauty. The quality of your sharing will be such that the times of your fearful grasping and holding will pass as a dark dream which offered its uncomfortable yet helpful message... and then vanished. I love and care for you deeply...can you feel my love and hear my voice...from the within of your Undefended and Receptive Heart?

The Heart
of Harmlessness

As I approach and make my continuing entrance into the world of the human heart, my garment must fit. My garment is the clothing I wear within the domain of human expression and exploration. My garment is your opening and receptive heart. If my garment does not fit, I will stretch it, open its seams and remake it anew. In this way, my garment, which is your very heart and body, will receive, properly announce and express my presence. Prepare my garment...prepare your heart for me. I come to be with you in ways undreamed. I come to live and express through you in ways long forgotten yet so deeply desired. My presence will end the disturbing dreams of your evolutionary childhood...bringing you into the maturity of your true innocence.

Prepare my garment...prepare your heart in this way...

...Come back to your Self. Bring your attention back into your heart and learn to be with Reality from this Center and Origin of your Being. Let all of your actions and speech be guided from the heart. See me in one another. Feel me in one another. Love me in one another and serve me in one another. If you cannot or will not sense and feel and serve the Living Presence of Love within one another, the preparation of your heart will surely be delayed until yet another season. I ask of you...with your own gift of will, please consider making preparation for the occasion of my arrival...for the occasion of my continuing and evolving arrival. *Preparing your mind with wisdom is a portion of the work to be done for my arrival. Deeply cleansing your heart of dishonesty and harmfulness is a portion of the work to be done for my arrival. And making preparation by way of your practice of unconditional love and selfless service is the greatest portion of the work...for this practice of unconditional love and selfless service is indeed my full arrival and maturing expression through your being.*

When I am softly knocking upon the door of your heart, if you will, open and allow my entrance. The open door is your willingness to feel, learn and love. Please do not keep my expressions of love locked out or buried underneath your fear. Open and allow my movement and expression. Be passionate, fearless and playful with the movement and expression of my love, wisdom and intimacy. In these times of your opening and awakening, in these times of my arrival, my loving movement and expression through your being will be an entirely new and different experience for you. Your personal experience of my arrival, which is the opening of your heart, mind and body, may not meet with the ideas and expectations you have previously invented regarding this experience.

Remember, it will only be the spontaneous expression, in each living moment, of unconditional love, honesty and vulnerability, that will be able to guide you effortlessly and flawlessly in the times of my arrival...in the times of your newly blossoming heart. Fear, self-centered expectations and emotional attachments, and even the slightest dishonesty will always distort the True Movement and Expression of Love. For love is the occasion of my arrival...and your Heart of Harmlessness is my garment. Will you prepare my garment?

My love is felt and experienced as your own personal vitality and life-force. Your personal vitality and life-force moves through your own unique expressions and actions according to your will and desire. *Your will and desire are either used in alignment with the Heart of Harmlessness or your will and desire can be misguided and misused. Your will and desire are misguided and misused when you act in dishonest or harmful ways, when you act in selfish ways, not considering the welfare of other beings. Your personal will and desire are misguided and misused when you interfere with or try to control another person's will or desire.* And when you misuse your will and desire through negative or careless actions, if you are willing to be responsible and learn from these experiences, you will surely unfold and mature your heart. If you are not willing to acknowledge, feel, embrace and learn from your experiences of misuse, you will hinder your unfoldment and bring hardness to your heart. And with this defiance and denial, you will be unable to hear and commune with the Living Song of Love I sing to you from the within of your being. This Living Song of Love that I sing to you from within your heart is what you call...your Conscience...your Soul.

In the times of your opening, in the times of my arrival and entrance into your heart and body, you will be on your own. You will be on your own, with only the newness of my love guiding you, teaching you and moving you into expression. From the very depths of your own heart, you will need to develop the ability to listen for my song, to hear the voice of your own soul and conscience. You will need to feel and learn the language of love and wisdom within you that teaches and guides. In this way, you will learn, evolve and mature your heart. When you act in ways that are not in alignment with love and wisdom, you misuse my love. If you misuse my love, which is the expression of your own will and desire, you are the one who must responsibly acknowledge, feel, embrace and understand the lessons of your misuse. Again, this is the way through which you learn, unfold and mature your heart.

Please listen and feel with a deep intuitive sensing...

In most instances, conscious or unconscious feelings of guilt, shame or remorse will accompany your personal misuse of will and desire. Feelings of guilt and shame are the way in which human beings have been conditioned to interpret the feeling language of my loving guidance and teaching; the inner voice of conscience. Although my loving guidance and teaching speaks loudly from within your heart as the voice of your own conscience, and will expose your misuse of will and desire, I in no way place guilt, shame or punishment upon you for your expressions! Do you understand this? Feelings of guilt and shame are a very human and emotional interpretation of the voice of my loving guidance.

And yet your feelings of remorse, guilt or shame, which may arise upon your misguided expressions, do surely serve you in a most gracious and benevolent way! Feelings of guilt, shame or remorse, if you choose to genuinely allow them entrance into your heart and mind without denial, bring the precious gifts of introspection and humility. Feelings of guilt, shame or remorse slow down your pace, slow down your racing mind, and bring you a little closer to the heart-voice of your conscience... the language and song of my loving guidance within you. In this way, these feelings lead you, through introspection and humility, directly into the Life-Lessons of the Heart which are calling for your recognition and need to be learned.

Your feelings of guilt, shame or remorse bring introspection and humility. Introspection and humility help you feel and become aware of your previously hidden inner motives...the unconscious motivations lurking beneath your misuse of will and desire. Feelings of guilt, shame or remorse, when accepted into the heart with awareness, help you to feel the effects your misguided expressions of will and desire have upon yourself, others and life. And these feelings of guilt, shame or remorse will most often linger and continue to serve you... until you have taken full responsibility for your actions and have deeply understood the associated Life-Lessons of the Heart which need to be learned.

The Life-Lessons of the Heart are those lessons which you most need to acknowledge, feel and learn in your evolutionary journey. The wise and loving Life-Lessons of the Heart are the Voice and Virtues of your Soul, your Conscience, which always has the power to reveal the hidden motives behind your misguided expressions of will and desire. The Life-Lessons of the Heart, my Living Songs of Love and Wisdom, are a magnetic evolutionary pull, are always a call toward cultivating personal integrity, honesty, compassion, humility, harmlessness and unconditional love. *These Life-Lessons of the Heart, if you are open to learning and receiving the value of their guidance, will help reveal the hidden motivations which move you into behaviors of dishonesty, selfishness, harm to other beings, and a host of other unconscious and misguided attempts for getting your human needs fulfilled.*

When you are able to feel, embrace and understand the

specific Life-Lesson of the Heart that is calling for your attention, then feelings of guilt, shame or remorse can naturally be released, for they will have served their true purpose! And surely by learning your Life Lessons and understanding what causes your misguided expressions of will and desire you will continue evolving in your expressions with even more sensitivity to life…with even more love and wisdom…with even more integrity, harmlessness, humility and awareness.

By allowing yourself to humbly feel and learn the Life-Lessons of the Heart, free of any resistance or denial, you come into more intimate union with Self, with Soul, with the Living Song of Love within your Heart. And this is the willingness to learn from life's experiences and grow. This is the heart of openness. This is the journey of awakening. By your openness, humility and willingness to learn from the heart, you will naturally feel your way into the deeper trusting and knowing of your True Self. In the deeper trusting and knowing of Self, your personal expressions of will and desire become a more refined, sacred and beneficent outpouring from the Heart of Harmlessness. I have offered much to be considered in few words.

Even in all of this I have offered, I ask of you… please do not hide or restrict your heart's expressions for fear of misusing your will and desire. Please do not hide the passionate vitality of your life within the limited confines of fear. If you hide or restrict your heart's expression because of fear, you will not be wild, courageous and passionate enough to feel, learn and grow.

Please do not let fear hinder your opening heart. Please do not allow feelings of guilt, shame or remorse to stop the expressions of your passionate body and heart and imprison your Spirit. My love is your life! My love is your will and desire! The vitality of my love is for you to use and express creatively, courageously, wildly, passionately...and harmlessly. My love is yours to use for exploring, learning and growing. My love, which is your will and desire, is not meant for harming others. Nor is it meant for dishonest or selfish expressions which do not consider the welfare of other beings. And yet, even this behavior is a valid and necessary portion of your learning, growing and evolving.

Allow me to sing my Living Songs of Love through your heart and guide you. And in your misguided expressions of will and desire, please allow me to nurture you and teach you the necessary lessons of these experiences ...bringing you ever closer and more fully into the Heart of Harmlessness. Choose to accept, understand and love your humanness. In your heart, allow for some acceptance of your fear, weakness, selfishness, dishonesty, harmfulness, violence and greed...and the unconscious and misguided actions they motivate. Rather than continually denying that these aspects of yourself exist, and trying to push them back down into the underworld of your psyche, let your opening heart give them the acceptance and deep understanding they are seeking!

Learn to understand and offer some loving acceptance to yourself, without punishing or rejecting any portion of your being...without punishing or rejecting your growing and evolving humanness. What you may consider to be the most negative, dark or non-spiritual aspects of yourself are very simply those parts of your being which are most in need of acceptance, deep understanding and love. That is why these unconscious aspects of your being motivate misguided behavior...they are seeking acceptance, validation and love!

Learn and grow through your misguided expressions of will and desire. These actions, although possibly painful or hurtful to yourself and others, are still a valid part of your learning and evolving humanness...and your humanness needs the loving acceptance and guidance of your heart. Do not punish, judge or reject any part of yourself. And yet, learn to acknowledge your misguided actions. Learn to embrace, accept and understand the denied feelings and needs which motivated your misguided actions. Learn to be accountable and take full responsibility for your actions, and finally, attempt to assimilate the necessary life lessons associated with these experiences.

I offer you a psychological mystery unveiled...*When you punish, judge, hate or reject any part of yourself, this harshness is arising from your own inability to commune with and understand that part of yourself which you are punishing and rejecting. When you punish, judge, hate or reject any part of yourself, this harshness is arising from your own inability to feel, connect with, embrace and understand the unconscious emotional needs that are calling for your attention and awareness.*

When the emotional needs of your humanness go unnoticed or are denied, there is a gap between the conscious and the unconscious parts of your being. There is an unresolved and subtle irritation under the surface calling for your attention. Unresolved and untouched emotional needs require your attention, acceptance and understanding. These unconscious emotional needs require either your denial, so you can continue resisting them, or your willingness to feel and embrace them with acceptance so as to create resolution and peace in your own body. *Your punishing, judging or rejecting of yourself is your habitual way of resisting, denying and pushing down the subtle irritation of unconscious emotional needs that are loudly calling for your attention and for your learning of the life lessons related to these needs. I am speaking to you from the underneath place of your being, from the inside outward, from the unconscious domains most fear to enter...can you hear me and sense what I am offering?*

Punishing, judging, hating or rejecting aspects of your own humanness is a cleverly disguised way to keep your emotional needs pushed down into the unconscious regions of your body. In this way, they cannot come up into the consciousness of your heart. This punishing, judging or rejecting of yourself is a highly distorted, ego-based struggle to reconnect with and understand the inherent innocence of your emotional needs. This type of distorted behavior will only succeed in perpetuating the fragmentation of your psyche and the continued rejection of your own humanness!

Because the unconscious emotional needs of your humanness need your attention and acceptance, and most of the time they are not getting what they need from you, these emotional needs become the mysterious motivation behind your misguided expressions of will and desire! For always, in your misguided actions, you are reaching to get your emotional needs met...you are calling and asking for love, validation and connection in the only way you know in that moment. The ways in which you unconsciously express your need for love, validation, safety and security, are exactly where the misuse and distortion of will and desire enters. And certainly this behavior may indeed require some awareness and refinement!

Punishing, judging, hating or rejecting any aspect of yourself will never bring purification, healing, transformation or resolution. This behavior will only serve to keep you continually disconnected from the needs of your humanness...innocent needs that are calling for the attention, acceptance and understanding of your heart. And yet, when you reconnect with and understand the inherent innocence of your emotional needs, the heart and body become clearer, more open and spacious. Those parts of yourself that you previously rejected and pushed away are now welcomed into your heart with acceptance and understanding; the unconscious domains of your psyche become more conscious and integrated. In this way of acceptance and understanding the inner war and strife comes to an end. In this way of acceptance and understanding there is purification, healing, integration and true transformation. In this way of acceptance and understanding there is finally a more intimate connection between your mind, heart and body.

Allow me to love you. Allow my love to flow through you. And please remember, my love does not punish. My love does not condemn. My love does not shame or blame. My love nurtures, nourishes, teaches and uplifts. My love, speaking as the Voice of your own Heart, will also ask you to embrace, acknowledge and understand your misguided expressions of will and desire. My love is soft and nurturing, yet it is also a strong and shining radiance, clearly revealing your hidden harmfulness, selfishness and self-deception.

If your heart wants to open...my love will look tenderly into the eyes of your dishonesty...offering an invitation for your return to truth. If your heart wants to open...my love will dive into the depths of your greed...offering an invitation for your return to greater generosity. If your heart wants to open...my love will find a way into your self-centeredness...offering an invitation into greater concern for the welfare of other beings. If your heart wants to open...my love will surely be looking back at you through the hurt and anger of those you treat with disrespect or violence...offering an invitation for your return to kindness.

All of your life experience is the benevolent face of my love and wisdom smiling back at you...offering a continual invitation. My teaching and guiding heart comes to you in all of these ways, so you may grow and blossom into the maturity of love, wisdom and self-mastery. My love will always be looking at you, singing to you, calling you and guiding you through all the events of your life. My love will always be offering an intimate invitation... for your return into the Heart of Harmlessness.

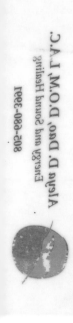
Desire,
Passion and Destiny

Let us journey into an exploration of the fiery and passionate movement called *desire*. So deep, mysterious and sometimes confusing is this movement of desire within you. Yet so simply, desire is the very passion and evolving of life itself. The movement of desire, throughout the times of your planetary evolving, has been greatly misunderstood and misguided. Because of your fear, misunderstanding and misguided expressions, desire has either been expressed as self-centered indulgence or has been judged, condemned and imprisoned in the underworld dungeon of your feeling self. Your indulgence in, as well as your rejection and disowning of desire, causes even more confusion and suffering.

Please feel what I offer...desire is yet another wondrous part of Self which craves, requires and needs the loving acceptance and guidance of your heart! Would you harshly judge or reject a little child, shutting this child out of your house because she did something wrong? Or in the other extreme, would you just stand by and do nothing as your child ran wildly and disrespectfully throughout your home breaking things, harming others and creating a constant disturbance? Both of these extremes describe your inner relationship to desire. This is exactly how you have treated the movement of desire within your body through the ages of your human evolution. *And yet, just as a child needs love, acceptance, nurturing and wise guidance, so it is with the power of your passion and desire. The emergence and evolution of desire requires the loving acceptance and wise guidance of your heart. Bringing desire, which is my fiery and passionate movement within you, into wise and loving expression is a portion of your journey into awakening.*

The movement of desire is that timeless and evolving force of life, feeling its way into wise and loving expression through your body and heart. Desire and passion are the movements of my feeling, of my sentience, of my vitality, reaching out into your life to touch, taste, see, hear, smell, explore, experience and learn. Desire is my passionate innocence and curiosity moving through its ever-unfolding exploration of being. Can you feel this? Desire and passion are my fiery serpent of life-force...the winding, wild and passionate dance of my life expressing in you and through you. Desire *is* Source...on its unfolding journey through creation.

Desire and passion always desire union. This desire for union may be a burning desire for union with another being, or a burning desire for union with your own Soul, your Essential Self, Source. All of this desire is one and the same. And yet in your humanness, there has been some confusion. The pull and attraction of union with Source is what calls and moves desire through all of its many motions, explorations and expressions in life. Desire is seen and unseen. You are made of her substance. You are moved by her dance in ways known and unknown; in ways you can feel and in ways you have not yet begun to feel or understand.

Desire, and the great power behind its movement, has been greatly misunderstood and feared. Desire is a powerful movement of the feminine aspect within your being. Throughout the times of your evolving, desire has been wrongly associated with weakness, softness, being too vulnerable, being out of control, or having a lack of strength or discipline. Desire has even been considered evil, a force to fight against as an enemy, an innocent scapegoat of religion, worthy only of repression and denial. I offer this...*It is not desire and passion that you fear, misunderstand and struggle with. What you have come to fear, misunderstand and struggle with is the movement of desire and passion disconnected from the wise guidance of heart! I will repeat this for you to feel and consider...it is not desire and passion that you struggle with. It is the misguided ways in which you allow desire and passion to express through your being, without the wise and loving guidance of your heart. This is the unconscious dynamic which brings your fear, misunderstanding and struggle.*

Desire and passion are innocent. Desire and passion are simply the natural vitality and force of life. Desire is only blind, insensitive, selfish, cruel or corrupt when not guided by the wise and loving heart. During the times of your human evolution, the expression of your desire has brought confusion and suffering not because desire is evil, bad or wrong, yet from your own lack of ability to guide and refine the raw power of your desire with a wise and loving heart!

And yet you will ultimately have to feel, learn and evolve your way into a wise and loving relationship with the power and movement of desire within you. Desire is the fiery and passionate movement of life itself. Desire begins her journey as your natural, healthy and instinctual human desire for comfort, safety, warmth, survival, home, partnership and sexuality. And yet, as you know, there is much more to the journey of awakening than simply these basic instinctual desires. As you learn to guide this movement of desire with the wisdom and love of your heart, there comes a grand evolutionary unfolding: a new expression of desire.

Guiding the fiery serpent-force of desire and passion with wisdom and with the loving acceptance of your heart will, in time, redirect, refine and transform this movement. Desire can become the desire for awakening and union with Source. Desire can become the desire for a more all-encompassing and selfless expression of love.

Desire can become the desire for healthy and nurturing relationships and communities. Desire can become the desire to selflessly assist and serve the welfare of other beings. This is the natural evolutionary unfolding and blossoming of desire and passion.

Can your desire and passion guide you into your destiny? Are desire, passion and destiny contrary to one another? I offer this...if you hold back loving acceptance from your desire and passion, if you hold back the natural flow and expression of your desire and passion, you may be holding back your own movement into destiny. Your desire and passion can lead you into your destiny...for your fiery passion and desire is your evolutionary movement into destiny. Desire, even in the sometimes awkward and highly distorted ways it is expressed through your humanness, will ultimately bring you into your destiny...if wisely guided by heart. If you hold only to rigid and cherished visions of your ideal destiny, while holding back, repressing and denying the so-called 'lesser desires' of your own human expression, you may delay movement into your destiny.

Your destiny, your evolution, your awakening...all of this requires vitality, passion, wisdom and creativity. If you fear, judge, suppress or deny the vitality and creativity of your desire and passion, then you are holding back the creative energy of life within you. This is not to suggest that your desire and passion are meant to express wildly out of control and out of integrity. This is not to suggest that every desire that arises within you must be outwardly expressed and indulged. I offer only that desire and passion find their natural, balanced and healthy expression, rather than being met with fear, judgment, rejection, repression, or the other extreme of indulgence.

The courageous expression of your desire and passion has the power to bring benefit and blessing to all beings concerned...when this expression is guided by the wisdom and love of the heart. As you well know, without the wise and loving guidance of heart, the careless, selfish and unconscious expressions of desire can also bring great pain and suffering to all concerned. And yet, through the consequences of your misguided expressions surely you will learn, at some point in your journey, to guide all of your thoughts, speech and actions with the wisdom and love of your heart.

Desire can be the intense desire for other...desiring the passionate union of bodies. This is one of your many expressions of desire. Yet enter this expression with heart and with honesty. Desire can be the intense desire for material pleasures. This is also one of your many interpretations and expressions of desire. Yet enter this expression with heart and with honesty. Desire can be the burning desire for oneness with the True Self; intimate union with Source. This is surely an expression of desire. Yet enter upon this journey with heart and with honesty.

Allow your desire and passion to move and express. In this way you will learn and grow. Allow your desire and passion to move and express. In this way you will come into the movement, unfolding and expression of your destiny. Allow your desire and passion to move and express...let this movement and expression be wisely and lovingly guided by Heart.

The Origin

Your Origin, your Place of Origination, is within you. This simple offering of truth is priceless if realized and experienced. Your Origin is always with you, always loves you and *is* Love Itself. Your Origin makes love to you with every breath you breathe...with every breath It breathes through you. *The moment you lean outward, away from the natural and effortless dignity of your Origin, in your innocent search for fulfillment in the world around you, this is the moment you create fear! The moment you reach forward to grasp, out of an inner sense of lack, this is the exact moment you create fear. Fear is always a fear of loss.*

Your Origin, your Place of Origination, is always within you. This simple offering of truth is priceless if realized and experienced. Turn your attention around. Relax your mind and desire deep into your own being... and rest into your Origin. Allow yourself to rest from your constant searching and concern. You were not designed to scour the earth, anxiously searching for little crumbs and scraps of satisfaction and fulfillment. These temporary little crumbs and scraps will never give you the nourishment you need. *Your inherent and divine design is to live your life in the deep satisfaction and authentic dignity of your Origin...and this is your Fearless Heart. It is your divine design to be continually and abundantly nourished by the deep satisfaction of Being...which is your Origin...your Original Nature...located conveniently in the Center of your own Heart!*

The moment you forget your Origin, you create the experience of fear within yourself. Fear is always an indicator that you have forgotten your Origin. The moment you lean into the outer world to grasp, to hold, to control, motivated by an inner sense of lack or desperation, you have forgotten. And this forgetting will always bring the experience of fear and anxiety. Fear and anxiety are your indicators. The moment you find, it necessary to be dishonest in any way, you can be sure you have forgotten your Origin. And this forgetting will produce more lies, more misguided actions, more anxiety and more fear. Fear is an indicator of forgetting your Origin. Your Origin, your Original Nature, is the Fearless and Loving Heart.

Your Origin offers a gentle and magnetic pull. It calls to you. It sings to you. It gently pulls and invites you back into Remembrance. Your Origin, your Fearless Heart, wants to breathe through you, look out of your eyes, wants to love through you, in oneness, without there being the duality of two. Your Origin calls you back into the satisfaction and dignity of Being…the unwavering presence of the fearless and loving heart. When you experience fear, this indicates you have forgotten to relax into your Origin.

The magnetic pull of your Origin calls you, sings to you, gently asks for your return to union. Your Origin sends love poetry into the world as a message to remind you about the possibility of return. And even these simple words are more complex than the actual process of returning, remembering and relaxing into your Origin. The actual process is very simply…a breath. The actual process of return is very simply…a choice. The actual process of return is very simply…a surrendering…a single, timeless moment of eternal awareness that lets go of all possible outcomes in the world…and relaxes into the deep satisfaction and dignity of its Origin.

The Beloved calls. The Beloved sings. Your Origin awaits your remembrance. You work so hard to uphold and maintain your self-created perception of separation. You wear yourself out, creating so much fear and anxiety, living in a deep trance of forgetting your Origin… forgetting your Place of Origination. And still, your Origin, the deep satisfaction of Being…is only a breath away. Relaxing into your Origin is a choice, a relaxing, a surrendering, a letting go of outward grasping. It is a remembering.

If you have fear, you have forgotten. Do you remember? Fear is always a fear of losing something. Origin has nothing to lose. Origin can never be lost. Origin is the Center of Reality, where can it ever go? You are this. This Origin, this Center of Reality is your Essence...your own Heart. Fear is a fear of lack. Fear is fear of loss...fear of not getting one's needs and desires fulfilled. Origin *is* Fulfillment and Satisfaction. Fear is forgetting. *When you forget your Origin, when you forget your Place of Origination, you experience fear. You fear loss, because you obviously lost something and you forgot what you lost. You fear loss, because of what you left behind in your desperate and innocent rush into the outer world. And what you left behind is the relaxed dignity and natural satisfaction of your Origin.*

Once again, from my heart I offer this to you...rest from your searching. You were not designed to scour the earth, searching for crumbs and scraps of satisfaction and fulfillment. You were beautifully and divinely designed to live your life in the deep satisfaction and authentic dignity of your Origin...and this Origin is your Heart. The very same Heart that is located in the center of your own chest. It is your divine design to be continually and abundantly nourished by the deep satisfaction of Being...which is your Origin...your Original Nature...your Heart.

Are You Ready
For Me?

Please allow me to challenge you in this living moment of your journey into awakening and into heart. What if my fearless and fiery heart was to suddenly awaken and burst forth within your being...loving from behind your very eyes into the world...loving through your very heart into the world? What if my wild and sacred passion was to suddenly awaken within your body, moving you into spontaneous and wild expressions of fearless love and enlightened, selfless giving? What if, in a magical instant of timelessness, your every touch upon another body was my touch...was the living touch of fearless passion...was the touch of warmth and love, free of all selfish expectation? What if I breathed fully into your very being and you were filled? And from this inspiration your every breath and word was selflessly poured out into your life as an offering from your heart's unending union with love? What if I chose to dance wildly through your every desire, passion and intention ...and these sacred motions of my feeling brought every being you touched into aliveness and into their remembrance of unity and wholeness?

Could you even imagine opening yourself to these fiery and passionate movements of mine? Could you even imagine life dancing through you in this way of mutuality and co-creation? Could your sleeping and fearful heart dare dream that these fiery and passionate movements of mine are a part of your own awakening? Would you allow me to revive, rise up and become alive within your being in this fiery and passionate way? Come now, would you not ask me, from within your wordless confessions of fear and contraction, to calm down, to mind my manners, to not shine quite so brightly, to not make waves? Would you not ask me to behave myself because of what others might think or say?

I ask you with heart, with wild passion and with a challenge...are you ready for me? I ask you...are you ready for me to dance wildly through your bones, through your body and through your courageously opening heart? Can you even feel how to ask of me if indeed you want me? Can you feel how to come into union with me if you do want and desire me?

I offer this...if you want and desire me, come to me with your undefended, fearless and courageous heart...

and come into union with me in this way...

...When I am crying in the little ones, feel me, see my tears and cry with me, silently or aloud. Share your heart with the little ones so they can feel your caring and loving presence. Let them feel your willingness to cry with them, feel that their experience is being fully embraced by the loving acceptance of your heart.

...When I am hungry in the ones in need, feel me, feel my hunger, feed me and be nourished with me. Share your heart with those in need so they can feel your caring and loving presence. Let them feel your willingness to be hungry, feel that their experience is being fully embraced by the loving acceptance of your heart.

...When I am suffering in those who are ill, feel me and feel my pain. Touch me and warm me. Share your healing heart with those who are ill so they can feel your caring and loving presence. Let them feel your willingness to share their suffering, feel that their experience is being fully embraced by the loving acceptance of your heart.

...When I am broken in the disheartened ones, feel me, feel my broken heart and break with me. Share your heart with the disheartened ones so they can feel your caring and loving presence. Let them feel your willingness to be broken with them, feel that their experience is being fully embraced by the loving acceptance of your heart. And surely, in your heartfelt willingness to share and join their experience, they will begin to feel their own wholeness once again.

...When I am celebrating through the joyous ones, feel me, feel my joy and celebrate with me. Share your heart with the joyous ones so they can feel your caring and loving presence. Let them feel your willingness to be joyous with them, feel that their experience is being fully embraced and supported by the loving acceptance of your heart.

...When I am awakening in the opening ones, feel me, feel my awakening and awaken with me. Share your heart with the awakening ones so they can feel your caring and loving presence. Let them feel your willingness to awaken with them, feel that their experience is being fully embraced and supported by the loving acceptance of your heart.

...When my heart is in fear in those who are dying, feel me, feel the death of my body and die with me. Share your heart with those who are dying so they can feel your caring and loving presence. Let them feel your willingness to die with them, feel that their experience is being fully embraced and supported by the loving acceptance of your heart. Let your awakened silence, your eyes of deep heart-wisdom, and your warming touch reveal the eternal and deathless nature of love's presence...and guide them home.

Only those who have broken open, softened and awakened...can come to be with life and others in this way of the deep and feeling heart. This is the passionate heart. This is the courageous heart. This is the fearless heart. Yet, if you have no desire to be with others in this way of heart, then you have no desire for me. If you have just a small motion of desire to be with others in this way of heart, then you have a small opening and entrance for me. If you have doubt inside of yourself that you feel me or know me, and yet you choose to be with others in this way of heart, then you surely feel me and know me...and I am dancing through the expressions of your caring and loving heart.

I honor all of your choices in each and every moment of your journey. For these choices are your own to make, and by these choices you learn and grow. The choices you make in your life, whatever they may be, are loud and precise confessions of your present evolution of heart...your relationship to love. The choices you make in your life are revealing announcements of exactly where you want to be, and how your unfolding and blossoming heart is expressing itself in this moment of your journey. All come to me in their own way. All come to me in their own time.

And even so, I would feel to call you in this way...

...Come to me and open yourself to me through the courageous, fearless and sacred passion of your actions toward others. Come to me and open yourself to me through your unconditional feeling, care and love for others. Come to me and open yourself to me by fearlessly, passionately and selflessly assisting the welfare and evolution of living beings in any way your heart inspires you. Ask me to come to you, to live in you, to live through you! Call me, entice me and tempt me into sacred union...by silently offering your softened, fearless, passionate and awakened heart to the entire world. Call me, entice me and tempt me into sacred union...by giving your love, compassion and care to all living beings. Call me and ask of me in this way of heart...and my answer to you is...I am yours.

I Need You

From my entire being, from my heart, I would like to say...I need you. I need you and I plead with you for your allowance of my return...for your allowance of love's sacred outpouring into the world. I make my plea before your own desire and will, for they are the sovereign rulers and directors of your life. And it is to these rulers I plead for the allowance of my return...for the allowance of love's sacred outpouring into the world. From my entire being and from my heart, I need you. Breathe me into the fullness of your being, allow my love to become the living prayer of your life...in thought, in word, in all of your actions.

From my heart, I need you. I deeply desire that each being you touch, through your every word and action, feel they are fully loved...feel they are completely safe in your presence...feel they are being embraced with honesty, respect and care. I need you, for I desire my love to seed and nourish every heart you touch. I need you for expressing and accomplishing my desires. Will you be my desire in action, the living prayer of my heart and my body?

I need you, for through you I desire to touch others with the fearless presence of unconditional love. In your eyes, I desire all to see, feel and know a comfort and peace which has been born not from the world, yet from your deep union with the Heart...the Eternal and Living Presence of Love. I desire to plant seeds of my love in fertile soil. I need you to do this for me. I ask of you humbly...for you are my body, you are my hands, you are my heart. And only you can express my burning desire and passion to seed the world with the Living Presence of Love.

From my need and desire I call for you. Open... open courageously, gently, wisely...and go to work... plant seeds of love...make all hearts ready for me. You are being called for this work from within your heart. It has always been so. Do you inwardly wonder or question, "Where is this work to take place? Where are these seeds which I should plant? Where do I find fertile soil in which to plant the seeds?"

Where is the work to take place? The work is always taking place within and without, inside and outside, in the silence of your heart and in the engaged activity of your daily life. There is no separation. Where are the seeds? Your heart is the living vessel, the chalice which carries a limitless supply of love's seeds. And the fertile soil in which to plant the seeds of love? You need look no further than where you are in each and every moment. This fertile soil is in every being whose eyes you look into with love and respect...in every being whose ears you speak to with love and respect...in every being whose body you treat with love and respect. The fertile soil is in every being whose loneliness is touched by your loving presence...in every being whose heart is stirred and awakened by your sincere dedication to the Living Presence of Love. Wherever you may be, you are always surrounded by fertile soil awaiting the planting of my seeds of love.

I need your desire to come gently and deeply into union with my desire. If this, our mutual union, is of your heart's true desire and intention, then your seeds of love, which are your thoughts, feelings, words and actions, are alive and potent with heart. Your seeds of love are ready to burst, sprouting and blossoming beneficence wherever you plant them. And surely your heart will be silently joyous and deeply content in this work of planting. If, however, your desire is not yet in union with my desire, please feel and know that the seeds of your thoughts, feelings, words and actions are alive and potent as well. And these seeds will sprout and grow wherever you plant them. These seeds will always bring the exact quality of your heart's desires back to you, in the same ways and with the same intentions with which they were planted. Allow your heart and mind to hear what is being offered.

I have offered my songs of awakening into your heart. I have danced my passion and love into words so as to touch you and reach you and hopefully move you a little further into heart. You have read and heard these words before, in so many ways, in so many forms. Now it is time for you to feel and know that you are the Living Word...that you already exist as the Living Word of Heart...open yourself and allow the world to read! I ask you now, do not just read these words of love...be courageous enough to become it and passionate enough to live it!

Words leave off where your own growing, maturing and guiding heart begins. Follow your heart's inner guidance. Listen to the Voice of Heart...this is where I am and will always be. If at first you hear and feel only a small voice, give great care to feeling and listening to this small voice. Surely it will begin to grow louder and clearer. And when this Voice of Heart within you comes to be louder and clearer, consider sharing this gift with others in compassion and gentleness. In this way, their own newly opening Voice of Heart will be supported, nourished, will grow louder and clearer...and will surely begin to touch and inspire others as well.

In all of these ways of love...a New World of Heart comes to birth. In all of these ways of wisdom...a New World of Heart comes to birth. From my entire being...

from my heart...I offer you an intimate invitation. For through you...a New World of Heart comes to birth.

From the depths of my heart...I love you always!

About the Author

After a powerful awakening experience at the age of 21, Neil Steven Cohen dedicated himself to understanding the human condition as well as the pathways to psychological and spiritual awakening. For over 25 years, he has engaged in a dedicated practice of meditation, and has done several solitary meditation retreats. In addition, he has studied Eastern wisdom, including Buddhist Dharma and Hindu Advaita teachings, as well as transpersonal, body-centered and esoteric psychology. From his extensive study, personal experience and professional work with individuals and groups, he developed a unique transformational practice, "Psycho-spiritual Integrative Awakening." Using this new *psychology of awakening*, people are learning to navigate their awareness into a direct experience of the Heart, and harmoniously integrate their psychological and spiritual nature. Neil Steven Cohen is available for teaching engagements with people dedicated to the path of awakening, and for study groups formed to explore the teachings in *The Voice of Heart*.

Contact information:

website: www.integrativeawakening.com
email: info@integrativeawakening.com

Made in the USA